MOVABLE HARVESTS

Dear Readers:

We wish you the greatest success in your container farming endeavors and would appreciate hearing from you about the successes and failures you encounter while growing various vegetables and fruit. Write to us in care of the publisher. Your anecdotes may be included in a future edition of *Movable Harvests*.

Good Gardening!
Chuck Crandall & Barbara Crandall

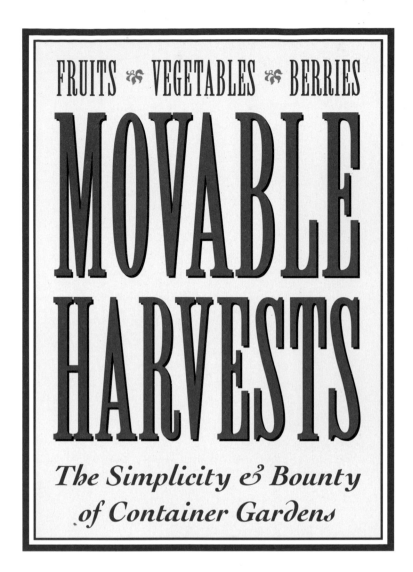

FRUITS ❧ VEGETABLES ❧ BERRIES

MOVABLE HARVESTS

The Simplicity & Bounty of Container Gardens

Chuck Crandall & Barbara Crandall

CHAPTERS PUBLISHING LTD., SHELBURNE, VERMONT 05482

Our appreciation to our agent, Kit Ward,
who shared our faith in the need for a book on this subject and gave
us innumerable constructive suggestions for improving it.

Published by
Chapters Publishing Ltd.
2031 Shelburne Road
Shelburne, Vermont 05482

Library of Congress Cataloging-in-Publication Data

Crandall, Chuck.
    Movable harvests : fruits, vegetables, and berries : the simplicity and bounty
of container gardens / by Chuck Crandall and Barbara Crandall.
        p.   cm.
    Includes bibliographical references (p.) and index.
    ISBN 1-881527-69-7: $29.95.—ISBN 1-881527-70-0 : $19.95
    1. Vegetable gardening. 2. Container gardening. 3. Fruit-culture. 4. Herb
gardening. I. Crandall, Barbara. II. Title.
    SB324.4.C73 1995
    635'.048—dc20   94-25239

Trade distribution in Canada by: Trade distribution in the U.S. by:
        Firefly Books Ltd.   Firefly Books (U.S.) Inc.
        250 Sparks Avenue   P.O. Box 1338
        Willowdale, Ontario   Ellicott Station
        Canada M2H 2S4   Buffalo, NY 14205

Printed and bound in Canada by Metropole Litho, Inc.
St. Bruno de Montarville, Quebec

Designed by Eugenie Seidenberg Delaney

Front and back covers: Photographs copyright © Crandall & Crandall

All inside photographs copyright © Crandall & Crandall except as follows:
Rosalind Creasy: pages 8-9, 25, 32.
Derek Fell: pages 18, 19 (bottom right), 67, 72, 75, 76, 86, 90, 93, 96-97, 107, 117.
Thomas E. Eltzroth: pages 64-65.
Walter Chandoha: page 112.

Contents

❧

Introduction

❧

WHEN WAS THE LAST TIME YOU ate a fresh-picked tomato? Remember how flavorful it was, and how tender the skin? That isn't just a nostalgic recollection. Tomatoes, carrots, corn and fruit all taste better (and are more nutritious) when eaten within an hour or two of harvesting.

Much of today's commercial produce has been bred to stand up to mechanical harvesters. Taste and texture are secondary. Because vine-ripened produce, such as melons, strawberries and tomatoes, is delicate and subject to bruising and decay, most crops are harvested "green" and shipped to distribution centers. It's common practice for some distributors to treat green tomatoes with a ripening hormone to turn them red. Although they are still not mature inside, they *look* ripe when they reach your supermarket. Melons that are picked green will slowly ripen in cold storage, but—while

they will appear mature in color, smell and texture—they will never taste as sweet and flavorful as they do when they're allowed to ripen naturally.

Corn is another story. Under refrigeration, it will keep for weeks, so it is harvested at maturity. The problem is that corn begins to turn to starch the moment it's picked. The longer the period between harvesting and eating, the tougher and less flavorful it becomes. Fresh-picked corn is so tender and sweet, it can be eaten raw or lightly steamed.

Sometimes with imported produce there is a more serious concern than loss of flavor. Because pesticide restrictions in other countries are often less stringent than ours, many growers abroad use pesticides that have been banned by the U.S. Environmental Protection Agency. As a result of budget cutbacks, only a small percentage of imported produce is checked for pesticide residue as it crosses our borders.

Much of the produce today is grown on corporate farms, where the primary concern is profit. As a result, prices continue to creep up each year, making fruits and vegetables an ever larger percentage of the weekly food bill. New gourmet varieties and organically grown produce are often beyond the means of most families.

But there is a solution to these problems. You can grow your own pesticide-free vegetables, berries and fruit, even if you don't have enough space for a conventional garden. You can raise a surprising amount of food on your roof, deck, patio or windowsill by farming in buckets, barrels, hanging baskets and other containers. In fact, it's much easier than plot gardening. There's very little manual labor, and your crops will mature faster and look better because you can give each the precise soil formula, fertilizer and water it needs.

To get you started, we provide step-by-step instructions on appropriate containers, planting mixes and fruit and vegetable varieties particularly suited for container growing. And we show you ways to make your endeavors as economical as possible. In each chapter, we give you money-saving tips, gleaned from years of container-gardening experience. We describe where to find and how to adapt inexpensive or free containers, which can reduce or eliminate your largest expense. We point out that while it's nice to have, you simply don't need fancy seed-starting equipment like poly cells, germination heaters and fluorescent lights. You can start vigorous seedlings in such common recycled

materials as milk cartons, margarine tubs and coffee cans.

You'll also find chapters that provide a thorough description of the diseases and pests that can

You don't need much room to raise fruits and vegetables. Even plums can prosper in a container garden.

plague fruits and vegetables and, more importantly, environmentally responsible strategies to minimize their impact and keep your plants healthy and productive. We'll give you tips on how to extend your growing season and even tell you how to raise exotic subtropical foods like guava and mango, as well as citrus fruits and nine different varieties of banana.

We think container growing is the way to go. Once you've tried it, we doubt you'll even return to conventional gardening. Get started today, and you'll soon discover what we learned years ago: You don't need much room to raise your own fruits and vegetables and enjoy the taste of foods picked at their peak of flavor. The rewards can be large, even if your space is small.

CHAPTER 1

Bountiful Gardens in Barrels, Boxes & Buckets

❦

WE STARTED GROWING OUR OWN PRODUCE ON A sun-drenched city apartment terrace many years ago. While our neighbors were adorning their tiny outdoor spaces with annuals and perennials, we were harvesting dozens of vine-ripened 'Patio' tomatoes and enough leaf lettuce and spinach for a delicious salad every night—all grown in about a dozen 16-inch flowerpots. This is when we discovered that freshly picked, home-grown produce has an incomparable flavor.

Today, although our backyard could accommodate a small truck farm, we grow everything from asparagus to zucchini, plus a large variety of berries and fruit, without ever turning over so much as a shovelful of dirt. We farm in buckets—and boxes, barrels and baskets.

We grow plenty of traditional produce, like lettuce, radishes and squash, but our favorite crops are the unusual (some might say bizarre) new varieties available, for the most part, only through seed catalogs. We soon discovered that there are dozens of new kinds of fruits and vegetables and hybrids of familiar types that never appear on supermarket shelves. Commercial-produce buyers are a pretty conventional lot. They stock only the foods they think most shoppers will want. On occasion, a few customers may take a chance on something like broccoflower. But how many are interested in a carrot shaped like a beet, a beet that looks like a carrot or a low-acid white tomato? We certainly are, and perhaps you are too.

You can order seeds for all the new gourmet vegetables from several different sources (see Sources, page 120) and start your own garden of unusual varieties. You'll probably find several you'll want to grow again and again for their unique flavor or appearance.

Of course, you don't have to grow just the odd or unusual crops. There are dozens of wonderful traditional vegetables and fruit trees, and some of them have been especially developed for container gardening. Recent introductions include 'Tumbler Hybrid' cherry tomato, which is perfect in hanging baskets, 'Bambino' eggplant, which grows to just a foot tall and bears 1-inch fruits, and 'Jingle Bells' bell pepper, which produces tiny, sweet red fruits that will add a wonderful crispness to fresh salads.

The diminutive crops adapt easily to containers, but you can grow *any* vegetable in tubs, pots or what have you, as long as the container's capacity is large enough for the plant's root mass. We regu-

larly grow standard corn in 20- and 30-gallon tubs and get an acceptable harvest, even though some nurserymen told us it couldn't be done. You just have to grow enough plants so that wind pollination can be achieved. We group tubs together, with four to six plants in each tub, and let Mother Nature take over from there. If you don't have room for standard-sized corn plants, you can grow one of the popular bantam types that require half as much room (10- or 15-gallon containers). There are only a few bantam varieties to choose from, but they all produce normal-sized ears with good flavor. From large plants or small, nothing tastes better than corn picked five minutes before a meal.

Container vs. Plot Gardening

One of the primary benefits of container farming is that your crops are less likely to be troubled by grubs, cutworms, nematodes, snails and slugs that are the bane of the plot gardener. These destructive pests are usually lurking in garden soil, along with a host of soil-borne diseases.

We get healthier, better-looking crops because we custom-blend planting mixes using steam-sterilized or fully composted ingredients, tailored to the needs of each crop. Then, we establish a fertilizing schedule for each plant's particular requirements. You simply can't do this effectively in a conventional garden, where everything is grown in the same native soil.

Another benefit of growing in containers is that you have a movable garden that can be shifted from one location to another to take advantage of sun or shade. Crops that bolt or wilt severely in the sun can be moved to the shade, and those that prefer maximum exposure can be positioned where they are bathed in solar rays all day or moved to follow the sun as it changes position through the summer. You can even trundle everything into the garage or under cover when a storm is imminent.

Don't overlook the savings in ointments and unguents you won't be buying to soothe blisters or

Pruning makes tomato plants more manageable and stimulates productivity.

an aching back. No longer will you have to turn over tons of soil, rototill in compost, manures or other amendments or battle legions of weeds just to get a few carrots or a couple heads of lettuce. Once you have mixed your soil, filled your containers and put them where you want them, you can tend your garden sitting down on a stool or chair.

In contrast to conventional plot gardening, only a few basic tools are needed for container growing. A trowel is essential. We recommend a one-piece aluminum one because it won't rust or break, even with continuous hard use and exposure to the weather. You'll also need a pair of hand clippers for grooming, pruning and harvesting. We prefer the bypass to the anvil type because it cuts cleanly without crushing soft stems. A short-handled garden spade can be handy, depending on what quantities of soil mix you will be making. Some container gardeners also find a light-duty hand truck useful for moving their pots and plants from one place to another. Other tools, such as measuring cups, can be borrowed from the kitchen.

It's extremely convenient to garden on a patio right outside the door so you can harvest a handful of green beans or a few leaves of lettuce for a meal without trudging through the back forty. With everything close by, you can keep a weather eye on your minifarm and quickly see if a crop is stressed from heat and needs a spritzing.

You can create colorful and handsome accents to enhance an entry, terrace or patio by combining in the same container such things as herbs (especially parsley, mints, basil and chives), lettuce, miniature tomatoes, strawberries and marigolds. Or you can put together interesting collections of leaf textures, such as ruby chard and kale, crinkly-leafed savoy

Container gardening can put fresh produce and flowers just a few steps from your door.

cabbage and spinach, or vibrantly tinged lettuce varieties, such as 'Red Sails', 'Rosy' and 'Rouge d'Hiver'.

By combining low-growing crops with climbers and viners, you can use attractive trellises to hold cucumbers, squash and melons and contrast these with cascading and bush-type crops like strawberries, limas, green beans and eggplant. Trellising not only adds visual interest, but it also maximizes container space.

The Benefits of Growing Your Own

One of the prime advantages of raising your own food is that you'll be treating your taste buds to a new sensation. If you've never sampled freshly harvested, home-grown produce, you'll be saying things like, "So *that's* what a tomato is supposed to taste like!" and, "Who knew a strawberry could be so naturally sweet?" Freshness equals flavor. Fruits and vegetables begin to lose nutritional value moments after they are picked. What does that mean for market produce that has been languishing in boxcars and warehouses en route to your town?

Besides picking crops that are fresh and nutritious, you'll be able to offer your family food free of the pesticides used by many growers here and abroad—chemical concoctions that are bad news for the human body.

There are several less toxic pesticides and beneficial predators that can give you a fighting chance against destructive pests without endangering your family's health or damaging the ecosystem. Many of these natural materials have been used by organic gardeners for years to minimize crop damage. Later on in this book, you'll learn how to put them to work in your container garden.

Container growing is a great way to introduce kids to the wonders of gardening.

Container growing is a great way to introduce kids to the wonders of gardening and get them interested in something other than the Teenage Mutant Ninja Turtles—at least temporarily. Children as young as four can (with some supervision) plant and care for a tub of mixed vegetables or sow a pot of radishes, which are quick to germinate and fast to mature. Older children, given a few containers of their own, can find a world of satisfaction in actually putting some food or flowers on the table, without feeling the burdens associated with tending a large garden.

The lessons of container growing can be just as valuable at school as at home. Raising lettuce or potatoes in the classroom can provide the focus for a whole curriculum on food and farming and on how dependent the world is on a healthy environment.

Overall, perhaps one of the greatest incentives for container gardening is home economics. You *will* save money on your food budget. When you consider what a packet of seeds costs and what you reap in return, the savings are evident. Fresh berries offer another good example of the investment-to-return ratio. A bare-root raspberry plant sells for about $2.50. A pint basket of raspberries at the store can sell for almost $4. You can harvest three or four times that many berries from your plant in one season and continue to do so for many years to come.

Food costs continue to rise each year. But by growing some of your own fruits and vegetables, you can insulate your household somewhat from these inflationary trends and at the same time enjoy the best-tasting, most healthful produce in town.

Getting Started

The size of your container farm will be governed by several factors ranging from your location and your available time to your enthusiasm and determination. First of all, you need an area with some sunlight. With very few exceptions, vegetables, berries, fruits and herbs need a minimum of four hours of direct sun each day, although most prefer six. The exceptions include the spring and fall (cool-season) crops, like lettuce, kohlrabi and broccoli, which seem to prefer some afternoon shade, especially if the weather turns hot. We've grown leaf lettuce in mostly shade, but it's always more productive with a few hours of filtered sun.

If you don't have a sunny area, you'll have to eliminate heat-lovers like tomatoes, peppers, squash, cucumbers and melons. While these crops may survive in open shade and even produce a few undersized fruits, they will always be weak, leggy and stunted.

Generally, the best location for your container farm is a south-facing site, which gets sun all day long, followed by a western exposure with 5 to 6 hours of sun, then an eastern site with 4 to 5 hours of sun. However, with some plants and in some parts of the country, the sun in southern and western exposures may be too intense and growers will need to put up shade cloth or move their containers in the afternoon. An exclusively northern exposure is usually unsuitable. There just

isn't enough direct sunlight for successful growing.

Even if you don't have an ideal location for a large number of containers, you can still grow on a small scale. In only a couple of window boxes, you can raise enough salad greens through the spring for two people and, in summer, switch to strawberries and miniature tomatoes. These crops prosper in hanging baskets too. So by putting up a few hooks and suspending a couple of baskets, you can "farm" on the window frame as well as the windowsill.

If your lawn or deck does not receive enough sun to sustain a broad range of crops, specialize in those that tolerate shade. Lettuce (especially loose-leaf types) is one, spinach is another, as are most mints and other tender-leaved herbs. We have even grown fine carrots and radishes in bright, open shade. So

A pint basket of raspberries at the store can sell for almost $4. You can harvest three or four times that many berries from your plant in one season and for many years to come.

A single squash plant can yield an abundance of produce for several weeks.

Second in convenience is an outdoor faucet close to your containers so you can leave a hose permanently set up. If you do not have a hose bibb where you want it, you can have a plumber install one. We had this done a couple of years ago for less than $100.

Costs are certainly a consideration when embarking on any horticultural project. With container gardening, there are a number of initial investments, including containers, planting mixes, tools and supplies. Depending on the scope of your endeavor, this may exceed what it would cost to start a conventional backyard garden. It may appear that you will be growing the world's most expensive tomatoes. However, keep in mind that you will have the containers and tools for many years. Likewise, the planting mixes can often be reused after composting them. Many of your seeds, assuming you have some left over, can be properly stored and planted in a second or even a third year.

A certain economy can also be achieved by using seed catalogs to their fullest. Most catalogues are free, and many contain surprisingly detailed information on how to start each type of seed—the optimum temperature, the number of days for germination and any special requirements to get it

don't be discouraged by a lack of direct sun. With a modicum of sunshine and a convenient supply of water, you'll be in business.

Planting mixes dry out rapidly because the sides of the containers are exposed. And most plants grown above ground transpire, or give off moisture through their leaves, faster than they would if rooted in a conventional plot garden. So when temperatures turn torrid, you may have to irrigate twice a day to keep your crops from dehydrating.

If you do not have a nearby source of water, don't be deterred. You can keep a reservoir of two or three 30- or 50-gallon garbage cans (or even 5-gallon buckets) near your containers and easily fill a watering can whenever you want to irrigate. Having to haul buckets of water or stretch out 100 feet of hose every day could take the fun out of gardening.

Probably the easiest way to meet your plant's water needs is to install a drip irrigation system (see Chapter 7) that can be operated either automatically or manually.

Swiss chard can be cut back or harvested a few leaves at a time, and it will continue to regrow.

to sprout. Catalogs may recommend soaking a seed overnight or "scarifying," or nicking, its seed coat to hasten germination. The advice given is very helpful. Container gardeners with limited space may also want to pay particular attention to descriptions of how tall or how wide a plant will grow.

When it comes time to make your seed selections, pick disease-resistant varieties. This can save you a lot of disappointment later in the growing season, when it is too late to start a new crop to replace one that succumbed to some common ailment. And keep in mind this lesson that we learned the hard way: You will have more successes than failures by choosing improved varieties (man-made hybrids) from established seed companies. This is especially true of tomatoes, cucumbers and melons, which are susceptible to a number of destructive diseases. Seedsmen, like Park and Burpee, as well as several lesser-known firms, are continually engaged in crossbreeding plants to improve their flavor, texture, productivity and disease-resistance. These hybrids are exhaustively tested in trial gardens across the country—sometimes for years—before they are offered to the public.

While we're on the subject of seed catalogs, we will offer these words of caution: Don't expect your vegetables to look as perfect as those shown in the glossy photographs. Seed catalogs, after all, are advertisements. The photos illustrate exemplary results, goals to reach for. So don't be distressed if your reach exceeds your grasp, at least initially. As you refine your techniques and discover your favorite no-fail varieties, your crops will look ever more impressive.

Even if your vegetables never resemble the "stars" in the promotional photographs, don't despair. We're convinced those plants were grown by a team of horticulturists whose only job is to get vegetables ready for their appointment with the photographer. We have yet to grow a tomato plant with

50 fruit per square foot of vine, or carrots that are perfect clones—each one fat, deep orange and precisely tapered. But every spring we are filled with optimism. We are sure that this year the photogra-

You can keep a reservoir of 30- or 50-gallon garbage cans near your containers and easily fill a watering can whenever you need to irrigate.

phers from Burpee will covet our vegetables for their cover illustration.

The first step in growing your own prize-winning, photogenic crops is picking the containers. This is thoroughly covered in the next chapter. As you will see, there are many options from which to choose.

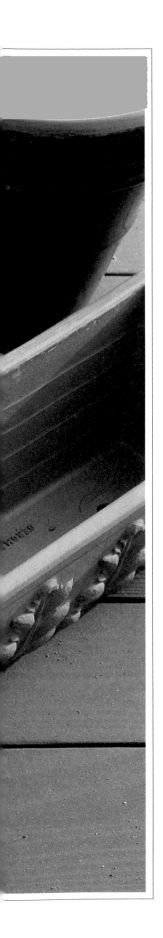

CHAPTER 2

Choosing the Right Container

❧

THE PRIMARY CONSIDERATION IN SELECTING A CONTAINER should be the amount of space needed for the roots of the plants you want to grow. How much depth and how much room do they require? The goal is always to give each plant just the area it needs and no more. You want to keep your container "farm" compact so you can grow as much produce in as many varieties as possible.

Some carrots will need only 8 to 10 inches of depth (Amsterdam and Chantenay types require even less) and can easily be accommodated in a 5-gallon pail, while many varieties of corn and tomatoes, whose roots can grow as long as 6 feet, will do best in roomy 15- to 30-gallon containers. However, there are some small hybrid tomatoes like 'Patio', 'Pixie' and 'Cherry' that do fine in 5-gallon containers and even in hanging baskets. Choosing appropriate containers, then, means knowing something of the growth habit of the fruits and vegetables you want to cultivate.

Where you are gardening may also be a governing factor in choosing containers. If you have a balcony or rooftop space, you may be concerned about weight. Your best containers will probably be those made of fiber or plastic, which, inch for inch, are much lighter than those of clay or wood. A half dozen large clay pots filled with damp soil can weigh several hundred pounds.

Aesthetics may also figure into your decision. Plants aren't particular about appearance. Any container that holds planting media and drains well can meet their horticultural requirements. But an old bucket or trash barrel will not enhance your patio the way an octagonal tub of clear redwood might.

Following are the characteristics of many commercial gardening containers to help you make an informed choice.

Wood

For appearance, durability and insulating properties, you can't beat containers made of redwood and cedar. Even though they are in contact with wet soil for months over a growing season, they resist rot and can be used year after year. Unfortunately, their desirable qualities do not come cheap. A 5-gallon redwood or cedar tub costs about

By building them yourself, you can have beautiful wooden containers for about half the cost of buying them.

$20 to $25. Using them for a large container garden would make for some pretty expensive lettuce or tomatoes.

However, if you're handy with tools, you can have the beauty of wood for about half the price of store-bought containers. Buy the less expensive grades of redwood or cedar lumber (clear grain, kiln-dried, without knotholes or other defects, costs the most) and make your own using galvanized screws or nails to put them together. In fact, you can use pine or other less expensive woods to make planting boxes that will last at least two seasons before they begin to deteriorate.

One way to prolong the life of all wooden containers is to fashion a lining of landscape plastic or vinyl swimming pool material and staple it to the bottom and sides of the box. You can use trash bags, too, but they are thinner and tend to puncture more easily. Plastic and vinyl are both inert and will not leach chemicals. They will warm the soil, which, with certain crops and in cooler seasons, can encourage good root development. Some gardeners coat the interior of their wooden planters with an asphalt sealer commonly used by landscapers to waterproof retaining walls. But we cannot recommend this, especially in containers used for growing food. There is a risk that potentially hazardous chemicals may leach into the soil and be absorbed by the plants.

Fiber

Although made primarily of paper products impregnated with binders and probably intended for relatively brief service, fiber pots are surprisingly tough, durable gardening containers. As long as their drainage holes are clear and they are not sitting in saucers of water, they can be used again and again. However, if water is allowed to collect in saucers or in the bottom, they will deteriorate rapidly. One

Fiber pots can be used again and again, as long as their drainage holes are kept clear and they are not left sitting in saucers of water.

of their best features is their light weight, which makes moving them a breeze. They're available in troughs, bowls, pots and 15-gallon containers. They have good insulating properties, keeping the soil cool and moist longer than clay. Some gardeners object to their rustic appearance. There's no getting around the fact that they are homely, but compared with nearly all other containers, their cost-to-size ratio is very attractive.

Clay

Traditional terra-cotta pots are the most popular containers for deck and patio gardening. Because they are porous, excess water and nutrients can leach through their walls. This can be the solution to plants that are overwatered or excessively fertilized. All vegetables and fruit do well in clay—in fact, they seem to have an affinity for it. The one drawback of terra-cotta pots is their weight, but if the containers aren't going to be moved often or set on certain roofs or balconies, this should not be a problem. Clay containers are available in the widest as-

sortment of sizes and configurations, from 2-inch miniatures to monsters of 40- to 50-gallon capacity suitable for growing small trees.

Plastic

Just behind clay in popularity with container gardeners is plastic. It is inexpensive and long-lasting and holds moisture in the soil better than any other material. This is an appealing advantage because container soil tends to dry out rapidly as thirsty roots compete for moisture in the confines of the pot.

Because plastic is a solid material, it is important to make sure that you have ample drainage and that you water and fertilize moderately. Most edible plants thrive in plastic containers, but keep in mind that black plastic absorbs more heat than lighter-colored pots, and this may pose a problem for plant roots.

One way to use black plastic containers safely is to double-pot in them. Set a smaller pot holding the plant inside the black plastic container, and put

Vegetables thrive in clay planters, which can be decorative as well as fruitful.

Containers need at least one large hole in the bottom, covered with a piece of fiberglass window screen.

a layer of sphagnum moss or crumpled newspapers between the two pots for insulation. Moisten the material when you water the plant to enhance its insulating quality. You can also paint the outside of black containers with white latex paint to reflect rather than absorb the sun's heat.

Unconventional Containers

With an imaginative eye and a spirit for recycling, you can turn up dozens of suitable containers. Many of them can be acquired free or for a nominal price. Check bakeries, delis and donut shops for plastic buckets that may have held pastry filling, pickles or cheese. Ask contractors for empty drywall compound buckets. Look at produce markets or large food stores for wooden fruit crates and baskets. Half whiskey barrels, ceramic chimney tiles, flue liners and wire hanging baskets can also find a new life on your minifarm. Some of them may have to be lined with plastic or sphagnum moss (or both) before you fill them with planting mix. But with a little creativity, they can become spacious, first-rate plant pots.

Preparing the Containers

Before you set your plants in these newly acquired containers, you need to clean them and probably make some modifications to ensure efficient drainage. Water that collects in the bottom of a container can be the kiss of death for almost all plants—unless you are growing rice. It can cause roots to rot, and it can sour the soil and encourage mildew and other fungal diseases.

Make sure the containers have at least one large hole in the bottom. (Most commercial containers have between one and four holes.) If you're using recycled buckets or other unconventional containers, you'll have to drill your own holes. If you have a power drill, use a ¾-inch spade bit or twist bit. For containers with a capacity of up to about 20 gallons, make four to six holes in the bottom. For larger containers, such as 30-gallon plastic garbage cans, use a 1-inch bit and bore at least eight holes. If you don't own a drill, you can make holes in plastic by heating the blade of a screwdriver and forcing it through the bottom of the containers. Our guideline is the more holes the better. (If you line a container with plastic, be sure to make holes in that too.)

Traditional lore calls for putting a layer of crocking (broken shards of clay flowerpots or rocks) in the bottom of a container to improve drainage, to prevent the drain holes from being blocked by roots and to keep the planting mix from sifting through. However, we don't do this. We've found that not only does this add considerable weight to containers, but it also creates crannies to harbor beetles, slugs, snails and other destructive pests. We recommend, instead, covering the inside base of pots with a piece of fiberglass window screen or a paper coffee filter cut to size. Both are relatively inexpensive. A roll of fiberglass screening costs a couple of dollars and should provide enough material to last several seasons. You can even recycle screening by sterilizing it in a solution of 10 percent chlorine bleach and 90 percent water and rinsing it thoroughly before reusing.

Any used containers may be harboring disease pathogens and should be thoroughly cleaned before you plant in them. Scrape off soil and fertilizer salt residue (white incrustations) and scrub the pots with a stiff brush dipped in a 10 percent bleach solution, then rinse well. You'll want to wear old clothes, rubber gloves and eye protection for this procedure.

Before using them, new clay containers should be "seasoned" or immersed in water for about 15 minutes to allow the pot to become thoroughly saturated. This prevents the clay from wicking or drawing out most of the water the first time you irrigate a newly planted container. Seasoning should be done shortly before you fill the container to start seeds or set in transplants.

Clay pots can provide years of service with a

Clay saucers, like clay pots, are attractive and durable.

minimum of care. The life expectancy of fiber or wooden containers can be greatly extended by setting them on bricks or blocks of wood so that air can circulate under them and reduce the likelihood of decay.

Depending on where you establish your garden, you may want to put a saucer or catch basin beneath each container to hold water that drains from the pots. Runoff, especially if the soil mix includes manure, can discolor decks and patios. Even with catch basins, container gardening can be problematic on wooden surfaces. Condensation under pots and saucers may promote rotting. If a wooden deck is your only gardening space, shift containers around periodically and wipe up moisture before it has a chance to do any damage.

Most of our catch basins are standard horticultural saucers sold by nurseries that are made of either plastic or clay. You can buy thin clear plastic saucers, good for about one season, for less than $1. However, we prefer saucers made of thicker material that stand up better to sunlight and to the rigors of moving containers from one place to another.

Clay saucers, like clay containers, are attractive and durable. If you are gardening in clay pots on a wooden deck, we recommend ceramic saucers, glazed on the inside, to keep water from leaching through onto the wood.

As with containers, there are many unconventional things that can be employed as catch basins. Aluminum pie pans and roasting pans are a couple of inexpensive possibilities, if appearance is not a prime consideration.

Water can be easily drained from catch basins with a turkey baster or from small saucers with an ear syringe. That way, you don't need to lift heavy containers after every rain or watering just to dump out the runoff. Drainage water can be collected in a bucket. We don't recommend reusing the water if it has picked up concentrations of fertilizer residue.

Once you have chosen the right combination of container and saucer to fit the crops you want to grow, you are ready to fill them with soil and seedlings and start on your way toward a bountiful harvest.

CHAPTER 3

It's Not Just "Dirt"— Planting Mixes for Containers

%

THE COMPOSITION OF SOIL MIXES FOR GROWING PRODUCE is extremely important to successful harvests. Your planting medium must remain soft and friable, or roots won't penetrate it and develop properly. This is crucial if you're growing root crops like carrots, beets and parsnips. Heavy, compacted soils can cause these vegetables to become distorted and diseased.

Your mix must contain nutrients as well as amendments that hold moisture for several days. But it must not become saturated or mucky because roots will rot. Finally, it must be free of soil-borne fungus pathogens and predators (grubs, cutworms, larvae) that destroy plants.

This means that soil from the yard or garden not may be suitable for container planting. It may be fertile, but it still may be inappropriate for growing vegetables indoors. In the East, some garden loam is too acidic, or "sour." West of the Mississippi, it may be too alkaline, or "sweet." In many areas (southern California is one), the soil contains so much clay that roots either can't penetrate it efficiently or rot in it, since clayey ground drains so poorly. You can, of course, improve garden soil by adding amendments that correct these problems, but the resulting medium is still not as good for container gardening as the light, uncontaminated mixes you buy or make yourself.

Packaged mixes and amendments represent only a small part of your investment. A 2-cubic-foot bag of commercial mix typically costs $5 or less, and bags of amendments run $3 to $4 at most discount outlets. A

2-cubic-foot bag of mix will fill four or five containers of a 3- to 4-gallon capacity. So for best results, you should always buy or mix your own planting medium, blending the right proportion of ingredients to ensure healthy plant development.

Soilless Mixes

These planting media, sold under names like Jiffy Mix and Supersoil, are extremely light and ideal for balcony and rooftop gardens and for containers that will be moved periodically. Many soilless (sometimes called synthetic soil) mixes are composed largely of sphagnum peat moss and perlite or vermiculite. Vermiculite is a form of mica that has been rapidly heated to about 2,000 degrees F. Moisture trapped in the mineral turns to steam and pops the gray-brown rock into small spongy

Some garden loam may be fertile, but it is still not as well suited for container gardening as the light, uncontaminated mixes you can buy or make.

fragments. They absorb several times their weight in water and nutrients and help keep container mixes moist. Vermiculite has some magnesium and potassium, which are two elements needed for healthy plant growth. Perlite is made from a whitish volcanic rock. It, too, is rapidly heated until it pops into small kernels. Perlite does not absorb moisture but holds it on its surface. It is also good for aeration, creating minute pockets between soil particles so oxygen can enter the mix. Oxygen is vital to the survival of plant roots.

Peat moss is a bog plant harvested primarily from wetlands in Canada and a few northern states. Like vermiculite, it holds several times its weight in water. Ground fir or pine bark and composted redwood sawdust are also included in some mixes. Ground wood particles contain some nutrients, but their primary benefit is to give the mix texture and body and to provide a stable anchorage for roots.

Here are two popular soilless mixes:

U.C. MIX

13 cubic feet composted redwood sawdust
7 cubic feet ground fir or pine bark
3½ cubic feet coarse sphagnum peat moss
3½ cubic feet horticultural grade or sharp
    builder's sand
To 1 cubic yard of these ingredients add:
5 pounds dolomitic lime
2 pounds superphosphate fertilizer
1 pound calcium nitrate
(One cubic yard = 27 cubic feet. One cubic foot = 7.5 gallons. One cubic yard = 202.5 gallons.)

LIGHTWEIGHT MIX

2 parts vermiculite
2 parts perlite
1 part coarse sphagnum peat moss

Standard Vegetable Mix

If container weight is no problem, a standard mix containing some humus and sand is recommended. Compost is often cheaper by volume than peat moss or mixes already fortified with humus

Herbs may survive in lean, unimproved soil. But, like most plants, they prosper in a medium that has been enhanced with humus. Most prefer a neutral or slightly alkaline mix.

and other amendments, so you can stretch your gardening dollar by buying compost in bulk and blending your own mix.

But if you're preparing only a few containers, buy commercially packaged mixes that contain compost and other ingredients. The amendments you're looking for are perlite, vermiculite and peat moss, along with the compost. If only one of these is missing, you can easily add that to the mix.

Here's a standard vegetable potting mix, enough for one 10-gallon container (for larger batches, increase the ingredients proportionately):

    5 gallons fully mature compost (either commercially prepared or homemade)

    1 gallon sharp sand

    1 gallon vermiculite or perlite

    1 gallon milled (ground) sphagnum peat moss

Blend these ingredients and fill one-third of your planting container with the mix. To that, thoroughly work in 1 cup of 5-10-10 fertilizer (5 percent nitrogen, 10 percent phosphorus and 10 percent potassium) containing chelated elements. Then add the remaining mix.

Planting Mix for Herbs

Herbs are hardscrabble plants accustomed to surviving in lean, unimproved soil. But, like most plants, they prosper in a medium that has been enhanced with humus. Most prefer a neutral or slightly alkaline medium. All but angelica, lovage and mint prefer dry feet, so the mix must drain well. A mix that has proven successful for us in container herb culture is:

1 part compost
1 part milled sphagnum peat moss
2 parts sharp sand
If growing angelica, lovage or mint, add one part vermiculite to the recipe.

Planting Mixes for Fruit & Berries

Mixes for dwarf fruit trees need to be light-weight because these trees are best grown in 15- to 20-gallon containers. The mix should hold some moisture but not so much that it remains saturated. This means using a soilless (or synthetic) mix. There are dozens on the market, but you can make your own by mixing the following:

Citrus roots rot if there is too much free water around them, so a mix that drains efficiently is essential.

9 cubic feet sharp sand
9 cubic feet fir or pine bark
5 pounds 5-10-10 dry fertilizer containing chelated trace elements
1 pound iron sulfate
5 pounds dolomitic lime

Another good mix for container-grown fruit is described in Lance Walheim and Robert L. Stebbins' book, *Western Fruit, Berries & Nuts* (HP Books, Inc., P.O. Box 5367, Tucson, AZ 85703; $9.95). It is based on the popular U.C. mix formula. To make 1 cubic yard of this container mix, combine:

9 cubic feet sphagnum peat moss
9 cubic feet fine sand
9 cubic feet ground pine or fir bark
1½ pounds urea formaldehyde (38-0-0)
3 pounds single superphosphate (0-20-0)
1 pound potassium nitrate (13-0-44)
8 pounds calcium carbonate lime
5 pounds dolomitic lime
1 pound iron sulfate

Citrus roots rot if there is too much free water around them, so a mix that drains efficiently is essential. An ideal mix is:
2 parts ground fir bark
1 part composted redwood sawdust
1 part compost
1 part sharp sand

Berries need a humus-rich mix. Blackberries, currants, gooseberries and raspberries prefer a slightly acidic (pH 5.5-6) medium. A good mix is:
2 parts sphagnum peat moss
1 part ground fir bark
1 part well-rotted (composted) manure
1 part sharp sand
For blueberries, increase the peat moss to 3 parts.

Strawberries require a sandy, humusy mix:
1 part sphagnum peat moss
1 part well-rotted manure
1 part ground fir or pine bark
1 part sharp sand

We like to mix our potting ingredients in batches of more than 130 gallons at a time. We do the work outdoors on a thick plastic tarp, which helps keep the materials together and simplifies cleaning up. We dump about half of our soil materials in the center of the tarp—ingredients such as compost, peat moss, ground bark and sand—then put in the lighter amendments, fertilizer and perlite or vermiculite. We then add the rest of our soil constituents and mix all the ingredients together with a shovel by turning everything over about 25 times, until all the ingredients are thoroughly blended. Some people mix their potting soils in a wheelbarrow, which is fine. We just don't happen to like the noise of the shovel against the metal sides of the wheelbarrow.

We store our mix in 33-gallon trash cans with tight-fitting lids. Whatever the container, it is important to cover it to keep out rainwater and insects that might burrow in and nest. Each of our cans holds a sizable quantity of mix yet is still light enough to be moved around easily. And in green plastic, the containers are fairly attractive. We also like the containers because they make it simple to gauge how much soil we have left and to decide when it's time to mix up another batch.

When we are using a mix that has no fertilizer blended into it, we add the fertilizer when we are filling our plant pots. We usually fill about one-third of a container with soil, then sprinkle on a dusting (enough to just change the color on the surface of the soil mix) of a balanced organic or inorganic fertilizer. We often use a granulated fast-release 5-10-10 or 10-10-10 formula. Then we fill the pot to within about an inch of the rim. As you irrigate, the fertilizer will dissolve and permeate

the soil. It will be available when the plant's roots develop and need a nutritional boost. In fact, this may be the only fertilizer the crop needs all season. In any case, we don't add fertilizer, at least not ini-

You can recycle your potting mix by adding it to your compost bin. By composting and recycling, you cut your costs and conserve resources.

tially, to the top layers of soil. It can burn tender young feeder roots. (Vegetables, berries and fruits require different fertilizer formulas. You'll find detailed information on feeding crops in Chapter 4.)

Toward the end of the season, after you've harvested a crop, you can recycle your potting mix if your plants were not troubled by disease. If your crops were diseased, the mix may be harboring pathogens that could infect new crops, so discard the material. If the plants were healthy—and most likely they were—you can add the mix to your composter and use it in another batch of potting soil when all the material in the compost is fully mature, or you can reuse the old mix right way to grow a late-season crop. Just blend it in a 50/50 proportion with fresh potting mix. But before you do, pull out any roots that have worked through the mix and put them in the compost to break down. By composting and recycling, you cut your costs and conserve resources, and you give your crops a healthy medium in which to grow.

CHAPTER 4

Nutrition for Crop Plants

❧

FERTILIZERS ARE SOMEWHAT OVERRATED IN THE CULTURE of food crops. Companies that make and market plant-food products foster the notion that your chances for a bountiful harvest depend on frequent use of their fertilizers. This is largely hype. Crop plants—especially those grown in containers—do prosper with a little nutritional help, but their needs are nothing close to what chemical companies convey.

The goal of feeding crops isn't to make them bigger, it's to make them better. Growing oddities of nature, like tomatoes the size of bowling balls or watermelons that you need a forklift to get into the kitchen, is okay—if you're trying to get into *The Guinness Book of Records*. But bigger is not always better. Small tomatoes are usually more flavorful than larger ones, and normal-sized melons are often sweeter than oversized specimens.

Here's the story with fertilizer. Without the nutritive elements present in air, soil and water, no plant can survive. These elements are carbon, hydrogen, oxygen, nitrogen, phosphorus, potassium, boron, calcium, iron, magnesium, manganese, molybdenum, sulfur and zinc. The first three are supplied to plants directly from airborne carbon dioxide. The rest are available as fertilizers and additives, either from organic or inorganic sources.

Container plants need fertilizer more frequently than plants in traditional plot gardens because nutrients in synthetic mixes can be flushed out every time you water. Also, the mixes used in container culture are usually low in nutritive content. They do not have the nutritional reserves of rich garden loam. So, to grow healthy, productive crops, you'll need to feed them periodically.

Fertilizer Types

There are two general categories of fertilizer—organic and inorganic—and you can buy several forms of either type. Organic fertilizers are derived from materials that are, or were, alive, such as compost, manures, fish meal, bone meal, blood meal and soybean meal. Organic fertilizers help build soil humus, which, in turn, helps the soil retain moisture and helps plants break down and utilize minerals. Organic matter also sustains soil microbes and earthworms that aerate and enrich the soil with their tunneling and with their waste or castings. Organic matter is the central part of an important ongoing process of building and maintaining life in the soil.

Inorganic fertilizers are derived from naturally occurring minerals or synthesized through various chemical processes. Phosphate and potash are two important inorganic fertilizer materials. Urea formaldehyde, sulfate of ammonia and ammonium nitrate are potent inorganic, or synthesized, sources of nitrogen. Many inorganic fertilizers release nu-

A pH test will indicate whether your soil is acidic, alkaline or neutral and whether it needs amending.

trients very quickly to plants and are said to be highly soluble. Sometimes more nutrients are suddenly available than the plants can use and the materials are washed down into the soil or volatilized and lost in the atmosphere.

Complete fertilizers contain the three primary and vital nutrients, nitrogen, phosphorus and potassium (or potash). These elements are listed on packages by numbers—10-10-10, for example. This means the product contains 10 percent nitrogen, 10 percent phosphorus, 10 percent potassium and 70 percent inert ingredients. This listing order is alphabetical and standard. The first number always represents nitrogen, the second phosphorus and the last potassium.

Fertilizers may also contain the secondary nutrients, calcium, magnesium and sulfur, and the mi-

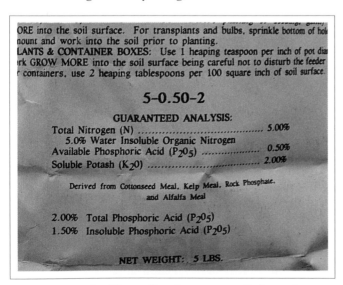

ORE into the soil surface. For transplants and bulbs, sprinkle bottom of hole
...ount and work into the soil prior to planting.
LANTS & CONTAINER BOXES: Use 1 heaping teaspoon per inch of pot dia
...rk GROW MORE into the soil surface being careful not to disturb the feeder
...containers, use 2 heaping tablespoons per 100 square inch of soil surface.

5-0.50-2

GUARANTEED ANALYSIS:

Total Nitrogen (N) 5.00%
    5.0% Water Insoluble Organic Nitrogen
Available Phosphoric Acid (P_2O_5) 0.50%
Soluble Potash (K_2O) 2.00%

Derived from Cottonseed Meal, Kelp Meal, Rock Phosphate,
and Alfalfa Meal

2.00% Total Phosphoric Acid (P_2O_5)
1.50% Insoluble Phosphoric Acid (P_2O_5)

NET WEIGHT: 5 LBS.

Complete fertilizers list elements on their package by numbers. This listing order is alphabetical and standard. The first number always represents nitrogen, the second phosphorus and the last potassium.

nor, or trace, elements, boron, copper, iron, manganese and zinc.

Nitrogen promotes the development and growth of leaves and stems and keeps the foliage lush and green. Phosphorus spurs the production of an efficient root system as well as bud and fruit development. Potassium is essential to the food manufacturing process and the formation of seeds.

Incomplete fertilizers contain only one or two of the primary nutrients. When they have only one of these, they're called single fertilizers. Blood meal is a single fertilizer, consisting only of nitrogen. Another is superphosphate, which is 100 percent phosphorus.

Single fertilizers are usually applied to correct a specific deficiency in a plant or to provide more of an element than is present in typical fertilizer formulas. For example, a phosphorus deficiency in foliage is characterized by dull, purplish red leaves, a condition that is often correctable by an application of superphosphate.

Fast-release fertilizers are either granular or liquid and dissolve easily in water. They release their nutrients (especially nitrogen) quickly so that plant roots can absorb them without waiting for them to be broken down in the soil. Most contain all the primary and secondary nutrients as well as trace elements.

Slow-release foods are blended with the planting mix in the bottom layer of soil and are also sometimes used as a "side-dressing" in which they are spread around on top of the soil and watered in. Eventually, they break down in the soil and feed plants continuously over a long period.

Timed-release fertilizers are made with a coating that slowly dissolves to release nutrients. Sometimes the terms "slow-release" and "timed-release" are used interchangeably, but while there are similarities in their actions, they perform differently.

Which fertilizer type is best for container gardens? We think fast-release ones are the most efficient. They are our choice for container crops because their nutrients are immediately available to nourish plants.

Some of our dedicated organic-gardening friends, however, consider chemical fertilizers the work of the devil. Actually, organics are more desirable in traditional plot gardening because they

ORGANIC AND INORGANIC NUTRIENT ANALYSES

NUTRIENT	NITROGEN (+/-)	PHOSPHORUS (+/-)	POTASSIUM (+/-)
Ammonium Nitrate	33%	0%	0%
Barnyard Manures*	1%	1%	1%
Blood Meal	12%	3%	0%
Bone Meal	4%	21%	Trace
Cottonseed Meal	7%	2%	2%
Fish Meal	10%	6%	0%
Guano	11%	8%	3%
Seaweed	1%	Trace	5%
Soybean Meal	6%	0%	0%
Sulfate of Ammonia	21%	0%	0%
Urea Formaldehyde	45%	0%	0%
Wood Ashes	0%	1%	7%

*Manures should be composted (also called "well rotted") before use.

*The proper amount of nitrogen stimulates
quick growth and lush foliage.*

You may be strongly tempted to give newly planted seedlings a bit of quick-release fertilizer to get them off to a good start. Resist this temptation. Freshly planted crops are in mild shock from having been uprooted and need time to recover. Giving them fertilizer may deepen the shock or burn their rudimentary feeder roots, which almost always results in the death of the plant.

After seedlings have become established in their containers (in about two weeks), you can give them a 10-10-10 soluble fertilizer diluted to a quarter of the strength recommended for flourishing plants.

The same rule applies to berries and fruit trees. Give them time to adapt to their new environment before putting them on a rich diet.

For both berry plants and fruit trees, you can use either slow-release or timed-release granular food mixed into the bottom third of soil or use two fertilizer tablets formulated for each type of plant. Over several weeks, irrigation water will dissolve the tablets or granules, and they will release their nutrients into the container around the root zone.

Recommendations for feeding soluble quick-release fertilizer are listed on the package label in the individual basic-care paragraph after the crop plant description. There are certain times when plants benefit most from feedings—a couple of weeks after planting, at flowering and at fruiting. Once you've grown a specific crop, you'll develop a sense for when it needs fertilizer to keep it vigorous, in good color and productive.

Not all the fertilizer you put into containers is absorbed by plants or washed out of containers when you irrigate. With concentrated inorganic fertilizers, undissolved salts can build up in con-

improve soil structure by adding humus, while chemical foods do not. Ultimately, a totally organic garden becomes so well balanced, you may not need to add supplemental fertilizer to grow robust, productive crops and ornamentals. But in container growing, the goal is usually to raise in a few weeks a bountiful harvest, not to develop organically rich loam for the future.

Some organic and inorganic nutrients and their analyses are shown in the chart on page 31.

tainers, which may endanger plants, especially long-lived fruit trees that remain in the same pot for two or three years. Every three weeks, you should flush out these residual salts by successive drenchings of fresh water—at least a couple of gallons per container.

Foliar Feeding

Plant foliage can quickly absorb nutrients and water, so spraying diluted fertilizer solutions on leaves will give certain plants a boost. Most often, foliar feeding is used when a specific nutrient deficiency is evident. Urea formaldehyde is the best source of nitrogen for foliar feeding. Orthophosphoric acid corrects phosphorus deficiencies and potassium sulfate supplies potassium. Sulfates of copper, iron, magnesium, manganese and zinc combined with citric acid and sprayed on foliage will correct deficiencies of each of these metallic elements.

Foliar feeding is routinely practiced by orchardists to provide a nutritional boost or to correct a diagnosed deficiency in fruit trees. Most fertilizer and sulfate products indicate on their labels when and how they should be used as a foliar spray. Fertilizers, especially those containing nitrogen, are used in a very diluted solution so that foliage is not burned by salts. If you are only growing vegetables, foliar feeding will probably not be necessary. When you will find it useful is in the culture of dwarf fruit trees, whose dietary tastes are more sophisticated.

The best time to apply foliar sprays is early in the morning on overcast, windless days. Don't use sprayers that have contained insecticides, herbicides or fungicides, even if you've cleaned them thoroughly. It's always best to have a separate sprayer for applying each type of chemical solution.

Finally, there are some basic rules that govern the use of fertilizers: Never feed a plant that is diseased or stressed by heat or, in the case of berries and fruit trees, one that has just been transplanted or that you intend to transplant in the next week or two. Feeding at these times can induce shock or may even kill the plant. Wait until the plant has had time to recover from any of these setbacks before feeding.

Foliar feeding is routinely practiced by orchardists to provide a nutritional boost or to correct a diagnosed deficiency in fruit trees, such as this 'Ein Shemer' apple.

CHAPTER 5

Seed & Seedling Savvy

❧

WHEN GROWING VEGETABLES, YOU HAVE TWO CHOICES for establishing your garden. You can start your own seeds or buy young plants. There are advantages to each approach. With seeds, you'll save money. Depending on the type of vegetable and the seed company, you'll get enough seeds in a packet that sells for about $1.25 to grow from 15 to a few hundred plants. Pony packs that used to contain six seedlings now often have only four plants, but they sell for the old price of around $1.30. It doesn't take a Mensa candidate to figure out the math here. Chances are you'll have leftover seeds so you can raise a second harvest or resow if something goes wrong with your first crop.

Another advantage is that many of the popular hybrids, new introductions and unusual varieties are only available in seed and perhaps from only one source: the seedsmen who developed them. So, if you want to grow these, you *have* to start them from seed.

Finally, seeds give you the benefit of starting your garden when you want to, so you can potentially raise more crops and harvest them sooner. We start seedlings indoors while it's still too cold outdoors to sow seeds directly in containers. When the weather warms, we have dozens of plants ready to set out.

Transplants from the nursery give you the convenience of having established plants you can set right into containers. If you've had poor results starting seeds, this may be the way you should go. Commercially grown transplants can give you harvests three to four weeks earlier than if you germinate seeds outdoors in containers, and by shopping early, you'll get the widest selection of varieties fresh from the grower. This may enable you to get two harvests in one season. Another advantage is that some of the varieties stocked by your local nursery may be types that do especially well in your geographic area.

But there are drawbacks with transplants. Your varietal choices are usually limited. Many nurseries carry only the varieties that have proven to be good sellers over the years. They don't want to get stuck with dozens of pony packs of yellow pear tomatoes or other novelty introductions.

Another problem with commercial transplants is that they are usually started in mixes that contain mostly peat moss. Once peat dries out, it is extremely difficult to wet again and keep moist. At some discount outlets, seedlings may be neglected and not watered until severe wilt is apparent. This drought-soak cycle weakens them by stunting their roots and limiting their top growth. Seedlings should be vigorous so they can endure transplanting and resume rapid growth. But if they have been ill-treated, they will be fragile at best and probably never highly productive.

Seedlings that don't sell right away sit in confined containers with their roots compacted, which further weakens them. Some, like broccoli and cauliflower, even begin to fruit prematurely, or "button," and will never produce normal heads in your garden.

Another problem is that the longer transplants sit on the nursery racks, the greater the chance that inattentive shoppers will damage them by rough handling or—and this is even more irritating—by pulling out a label to see what variety a plant is, then either not putting the label back or putting it in the wrong pack. Then, you come along and buy the mismarked pack. You may think you're buying broccoli, but you're actually getting cauliflower or cabbage.

Find out when your favorite garden center gets its deliveries of transplants and seed packets and get there the day shipments arrive. We do this every spring at a couple of nurseries and probably drive the managers slightly crazy. (I guess we *should* wait until the truck is unloaded and the merchandise is priced before we make our selections!)

Buying Seeds

There are two broad types of seeds and garden plants—hybrids and non-hybrids. A hybrid is the result of time-consuming and expensive cross-breeding and research in hopes of producing a plant that resists disease, achieves greater productivity and develops better uniformity. It may require years of testing before an acceptable hybrid is ready for the market and, even then, all the goals set by the seedsmen may not have been achieved.

Non-hybrids are also called open-pollinated varieties. Seed from non-hybrids can be saved and

Growing your own seedlings can give you a variety of plants you may not be able to find at your nursery.

will produce plants similar to their parents, unlike hybrids, which do not breed true from seed. Many types of non-hybrid vegetables have no resistance to diseases that may have plagued them since they were first cultivated. But just as many have developed resistance over generations of adaptation. Unfortunately, there is no widely available, reliable data on which cultivars can slough off diseases and which cannot.

We haven't had good success with non-hybrid varieties—especially tomatoes. Tomatoes are very susceptible to fusarium wilt and verticillium root rot. Many times, when we've planted non-hybrid varieties, nearly all of the plants have been infected with one or the other of these destructive fungal diseases, although it is usually fusarium wilt that gets them, slowly killing off leaves until the plant is almost completely bare. Rarely have we had this problem with improved hybrids, but it has occurred occasionally. Resistance to verticillium root rot and fusarium wilt is noted on the seed packet or transplant label as VF or VFN hybrid. (N means they are also resistant to nematode damage.)

Many gardeners remain devoted to non-hybrid varieties that have been around since grandpa's era because of their superior flavor. Manmade varieties of some vegetables lose their distinctive taste in the trade-off for better disease and pest resistance or higher yield. A secondary benefit of growing non-hybrids, as previously mentioned, is that you can collect seeds from mature crops and use them to start new plants. You won't have very good results doing this with hybrids.

Members of the cucurbit family—cucumbers, melons, squashes—easily cross-pollinate, unless their blossoms are hand-pollinated and taped shut or covered with lightweight fabric or the plants are isolated. Even though you may be growing only one variety, a neighbor may be growing a different cultivar whose pollen could be carried to your crop by insects.

Although we plant some old, or heirloom, cultivars, we prefer hybrids. We put a lot of time and effort into bringing our crops to maturity, and we like having the best odds for a successful harvest.

By all means, try some non-hybrids, but don't make them the backbone of your container farm. Consider your investment in time and materials and the fact that, if you use only non-hybrids, you may not have a harvest to reap at all.

As you might expect, hybridized seeds and pony-pack seedlings are usually more expensive than non-hybrid varieties, but the extra cost is worth it. Think of it as "crop insurance."

When you buy seeds and transplants and you want disease-resistant varieties (why wouldn't you?), here's what to look for on the label, in the catalog description or on the seed packet:

BEANS: MR hybrids—resistant to bean mosaic disease

CUCUMBERS: CMV hybrids—resistant to cucumber mosaic virus

MELONS: PMR and DMR hybrids—resistant to powdery and downy mildews

POTATOES: Certified Disease-Free

TOMATOES: VF and VFN hybrids—resistant to verticillium root rot, fusarium wilt and nematodes

WATERMELONS: TFW, An-1 hybrids—resistant to some strains of fusarium wilt and to one type of anthracnose.

Seeds are commonly sold cleaned and in their bare seed coats, ready to plant. However, very small seeds, such as those of carrots, are sometimes pelletized, or coated with a water-soluble material, to make them larger and easier to handle and more uniform in size for mechanical planting. Some seeds are also sold on strips of biodegradable paper. They are evenly spaced on the paper, which can reduce the need for thinning seedlings. But if you don't get 100 percent germination, you'll have gaps between plants. As you might expect, pelletized seeds and those on paper strips are more expensive than naked seeds and, for most container gardeners, not worth the added cost.

Mail-Order, Retail Seeds

The biggest selection of seeds is stocked by large mail-order companies, such as Thompson & Morgan, Park Seed Company, Shepherd's Garden

Seeds and others (see Sources, page 120). Order your seeds early (in late winter) to be assured of getting the varieties you want to try. Mail-order seedsmen occasionally sell out of a particular variety, especially new introductions, in their first year.

If you plan to buy seeds from a local nursery, try to shop as soon as the display racks are filled. Unless it is a very busy garden center, a store is not likely to restock until the following year, once a variety has sold out.

If you live in a rural area, you probably have a farmer's co-op or similar enterprise that either packages its own seeds or sells them in bulk. These outlets are a good source for seeds of vegetables that are acclimated to your geographic region. Although they are usually non-hybrids, some varieties are probably worth a try.

Another source of older, non-hybrid cultivars is the various seed exchanges around the country that are keeping heirloom varieties from becoming extinct. Exchanges offer seeds collected from their own fields or from like-minded gardeners who want to preserve certain particularly tasty, attractive or hardy varieties of vegetables and flowers.

One nonprofit group, Native Seeds/SEARCH (2509 N. Campbell Ave., Box 325, Tucson, AZ 85719; 602/327-9123), collects and distributes seed from ancient southwestern Native American crops that are in danger of extinction. They distribute seeds from their bank (over 1,200 species) free to Native Americans and also sell to the general public.

Once you buy your seeds, from whatever source, store them in a cool, dry place until you're ready to sow. We keep ours in snap-lock plastic containers in the refrigerator, but jars with screw-on lids work equally well. Just keep in mind that heat and moisture are destructive to a seed's viability.

Some gardeners collect, dry and sow seeds from crops they've grown. If this idea appeals to you, remember what we said earlier about collecting seeds from hybrid crop plants. Even those collected from first-generation hybrids won't produce the same improved plants. They may cross-pollinate with an inferior variety or even another species. Also, seeds often pick up fungal pathogens that can damage their viability unless you treat the seeds with a fungicide.

Having said that, we still think harvesting and planting seeds from healthy crops is an interesting experiment. Sometimes, the results are pleasantly surprising. You can get specific information on collecting and treating seeds from organizations such as the Seed Savers Exchange (see Sources). The basic procedures require that vegetables and fruits first be allowed to mature because the seeds and pits of unripened crops aren't fully developed. Remove beans and peas from pods and spread the seeds on old screens to dry for several days. Fruiting vegetables (such as tomatoes) must be ripe and on the verge of decaying. Then they are crushed, rinsed and spread out to dry. After a few days, seeds can be collected from the desiccated, pulpy material.

Before storing seeds, dip them in a solution of 10 percent chlorine bleach and 90 percent water or a drench made with 1 tablespoon of apple cider vinegar mixed with 1 quart of water, and spread the seeds on a paper towel for 48 hours. Turn them over once or twice to ensure thorough drying. Usually any residual disease pathogens are killed by these seed baths.

Wrap the seeds in foil, label each pack with an indelible pen, recording seed type and storage date, and place them in a wide-mouth jar with a tight-fitting lid. Before you seal the jar, place a tablespoon of fresh powdered milk in a piece of cheesecloth or nylon stocking and use a twist-tie to close the top. Set this in the bottom of the jar, seal it and store the jar in the refrigerator. Humidity and heat are the two biggest enemies of seed viability. Powdered milk acts as a desiccant, absorbing any moisture in the container. Change the powdered milk every three months.

This technique is also recommended for saving leftover commercial seeds for next year. Seal them in their packets with transparent tape. You don't need to place them in foil, but store them in a container with a tight-fitting lid. Don't expect a high germination rate for seeds saved from the previous season. In fact, due in part to many seeds' relatively short shelf life, you rarely get 100 percent germination from seeds produced for the *current* season.

To protect consumers from unscrupulous seed peddlers, Congress passed the Federal Seed Act, which regulates some aspects of interstate seed sales. The act calls for minimum standards of quality and germination. It also requires printing on seed packets the year for which the seeds were packed.

No one can say for certain how long a seed can be stored and still germinate. Properly stored seeds may have a 40 to 50 percent germination rate after many years. Others lose their viability after one season. We've found that seeds of beet, cucumber and

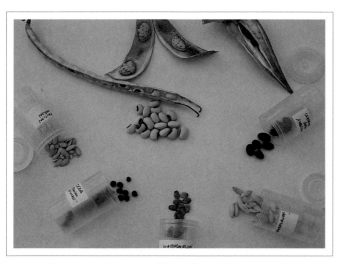

Some gardeners collect, dry and sow seeds from crops they've grown.

radish often remain viable for at least eight years; cantaloupe and watermelon will germinate after five years; cabbage, cauliflower, eggplant, okra and pumpkin after four years; bean, celery, pea, spinach and tomato after three years; and corn, onion, pepper and lettuce after one year.

Before you go to the trouble of sowing the seeds you stored from last season, you can test their viability by using a time-honored technique: Spread a few on a damp paper towel, fold the towel into thirds and slip it into a plastic bag or under plastic wrap to hold in moisture. Check the seeds in a week or so. If most of the seeds have germinated, you can be confident that the rest of the batch will too.

Starting Seeds

In the South (from Florida west to southern California), you can sow seeds directly in containers outdoors. But for gardeners in areas with shorter growing seasons, we can't recommend strongly enough the advantages of starting seedlings indoors. As we've said before, home-grown seedlings that are ready to transplant as soon as the weather cooperates give you a leg up on the growing season, bringing your crops to harvest three to four weeks earlier than if you started seeds directly in containers.

Frost-hardy seedlings, such as broccoli, leeks and kale, can be set out more than two weeks before the date of the last expected frost. Cold-tender vegetables, such as peppers, eggplants and tomatoes, should not be transplanted until about two weeks after the last expected frost unless they are given some protection. Most seedlings can be safely transplanted when they are four to eight weeks old. So you can decide when to start them indoors by simply counting backward from the time you would like to set them out. Information on the date of the last expected frost and the number of frost-free days in your area can be obtained from your local cooperative agricultural extension office.

What do you need to start seedlings? Nothing fancy or elaborate. You can plant seeds in almost anything that is deeper than 3 inches, has drainage holes and will hold the germination medium. Try using recycled containers: flowerpots, tin cans, plastic and Styrofoam cups, cut-down milk cartons and aluminum loaf pans will all work as long as they are clean and have holes punched in the bottom.

You can also buy peat pellets, which expand when soaked in water to create a container, and Jiffy peat pots, which we often use. Both types are good for seedlings that don't like their roots disturbed, such as corn, melons and most herbs. Roots can grow right through the porous walls of the containers, so at transplanting time, you can set the container in your outdoor plant pot without having to lift out the seedling. Just securely position the container in the soil mix and water well. The peat walls of the container will break down over the course of the growing season.

We've found that the best germinating medium for all seeds is a mix of one part each of milled peat moss, perlite and vermiculite. This is a sterile, soilless mix that is effective in preventing damping-off, a fungus disease that can either be preemergent or postemergent meaning that seedlings fail by wilting either before or after they emerge through the surface of the mix. There is no cure once this happens. You have to start again.

With almost any appropriate germinating medium, damping-off can be prevented by using sterilized seed-starting containers and sprinkling either perlite or milled sphagnum peat moss generously over the surface of the medium. Also, place containers where they get adequate light (bright enough to grow African violets) and good air cir-

You can plant seeds in almost anything that is deeper than 3 inches, has drainage holes and will hold the germination medium. Label your seedlings as you sow.

culation. Whether or not your seedlings have been struck by damping-off, don't reuse starting mixes. Mix fresh media for each new crop of seedlings.

When you sow your seeds, first wet the mix then drop the seeds at their recommended sowing depth described on the packet. Use a bulb sprayer or hand mister to irrigate until the seedlings are well established. If you're planting in flats, you don't need to be concerned about spacing the seeds precisely. A few days after the seedlings emerge, you can thin them. Snip off unwanted seedlings at the soil line with a pair of manicure scissors. Cutting rather than pulling out seedlings will not uproot the ones you want to save.

With large-seeded vegetables like melons, corn and beans, it is a good idea to sow two or three seeds in peat pots or milk cartons, then sacrifice the less vigorous seedlings so that one plant is left in each container.

Some of our gardening friends think thinning is wasteful. They let all their seedlings develop to 2 or 3 inches in height then move some of them to a larger container to give each plant more space. They prepare planting holes in the new container by poking a drinking straw into the soil, then they loosen the soil in the germinating flat and gently lift out the seedlings they want to relocate. Seedlings should always be handled by a leaf, rather than by the stem. Young plants can survive a broken leaf but rarely a broken stem.

Whether it is worth the effort to move some seedlings to larger quarters depends, in part, on how many transplants you want. It is always better to move them than to let them struggle along in a crowded space. But we have sometimes found that in trying to move seedlings, the ones we want to leave behind become tangled with the ones we want to move. We prefer our manicure-scissors method of thinning. If we need more seedlings, we simply plant more seeds.

Label your seeds as you sow. It's almost impossible to recall what you have planted where, once all the seeds are covered with soil. We use inexpensive Popsicle sticks and an indelible marker to record the variety, date planted and days to maturity. At the end of the season, we record in a note-book how each variety fared.

Seeds require moisture and warmth to germinate. Soil temperatures between 70 and 80 degrees F are optimum for starting most vegetables. Once the germinating medium has been moistened, never let it completely dry out. The ideal way to retain moisture in the mix is to cover pots and flats with plastic wrap in which you have poked a few holes so air can get in and some moisture can get out.

Vegetable seeds will germinate nicely on top of a refrigerator, where rising warm air keeps them cozy and hastens germination. Other potential germination spots are near (but never on) radiators and wood-burning stoves and in interior closets. (Most seeds will do fine in the dark until the new seedlings pop through the soil.) Electric horticultural warming mats and germinating coils can also give seedlings an extra nudge.

After the seeds have sprouted, remove the plastic wrap and move the seedling flats or pots to a spot that gets good natural or fluorescent light. Again, keep the mix moist but never boggy. Seedlings that wilt severely from dehydration seldom recover their vigor. Those that keel over from root rot brought on by soggy soil never do.

If you notice the seedlings leaning toward the light source, they're signaling a need for brighter, more uniform illumination. Be sure to give the containers a one-quarter turn every couple of days so that all the seedlings get adequate light.

Once seedlings have developed two true leaves, give them a boost with 5-10-10 liquid fertilizer diluted to quarter strength.

If you live in an area where cold spring nights and sudden frosts are the norm, you'll need to "harden off" the seedlings before transferring them to containers outdoors. To survive in a cruel world of desiccating winds, drastic temperature changes and intense solar rays, the seedlings have to be introduced to their new environment gradually. This is done by moving them outdoors to an open shade location (a cold frame is ideal) during the day and bringing them indoors at night for about a week.

We prefer the manicure-scissors method of thinning. It doesn't disturb our "keepers."

Keep an eye on them for signs of flagging. They may need water two or three times a day.

Once the seedlings have toughened up, plant them in containers, but be alert to frost predictions. You may have to cover them with protective caps at night until spring arrives in earnest. For one of the best cold caps, or cloches, cut the bottom off plastic quart and half-gallon milk bottles and set them over your plants when strong winds, heavy rains or frost are forecast. Under cover, they'll be snug against just about anything short of a hurricane or ground freeze.

If you're sowing seeds directly into containers, wet the mix down first, then sow. This avoids flushing the seeds to the surface, which usually occurs if you irrigate after sowing. Firm the mix but don't compact it. Roots have difficulty penetrating compressed soil. You want to encourage large healthy roots that probe deeply to firmly anchor your plants and efficiently absorb nutrients.

CHAPTER 6

Defending Your Garden from Pests & Diseases

❦

GROWING FOOD CROPS WILL INTRODUCE YOU TO BUGS and plant diseases you probably never knew existed. It seems that a number of destructive insects have the same affinity we do for fresh vegetables and fruit. No sooner do you set out healthy, young transplants than some voracious critter shows up to freeload. That wouldn't be so bad, if they didn't arrive with legions of their friends.

Maladies you rarely see in landscape plants, like wilt, mosaic disease and a host of viruses, can mysteriously appear to infect your prized mini-farm.

The fact is, even if you're gardening in containers, when you are raising fruits and vegetables, you may have some hungry insects and probably a few diseases to deal with.

Plant Pests

Most of the insects that attack crops are suckers and chewers. A few, like the cucumber beetle, also carry viral diseases that they spread to the plants they feed on. Nearly all insect pests are large enough to see with the naked eye. Mites, however, may be microscopic, and leaf miners do their tunneling between layers of leaf tissue, so you usually see only their serpentine paths of destruction on the leaf surfaces. Garden pests are generally "programmed" to feed on one or two specific plants and are often named after the plant they attack, as are the Colorado potato beetle and the cabbage looper. Others are omnivorous and feed on almost anything in the garden. Aphids are among these, as are mealybugs, slugs and snails.

Before we knew better, we were advocates of the overkill approach to pest control—the broad-spectrum, take-no-prisoners chemical pesticides. Then, we learned about the threat these lethal compounds pose to humans, animals, beneficial insects and the planet. Now, we take a more environmentally responsible approach when unwelcome invaders threaten the garden. We practice what is called Integrated Pest Management. Sometimes known as IPM, this strategy involves a combination of controls, including picking off

Tomato hornworms can be picked off and placed in a jar of soapy water.

damaging insects by hand, using insect traps, planting pest- and disease-resistant varieties and encouraging natural predators of garden pests. Another tenet of IPM is to avoid spraying any pesticide until you see some evidence of insect damage. You always try other, less toxic options first.

The simple fact is that, the more pesticides you use, the fewer natural predators, such as ladybird beetles, praying mantids and parasitic wasps, you'll have to help you. Many chemical controls are non-selective. They kill the good with the bad. Also, destructive pests often build up a resistance to synthetic concoctions.

Chemical companies have historically responded to this resistance by making their pesticides more lethal and long-lived. And some of these doomsday elixirs are with us for years, working their way through the soil, poisoning our groundwater, entering the food chain and, eventually, coming back to haunt us. DDT is a prime example. It has damaged marine life in many rivers and threatened some of our wildlife with extinction. Although it has been banned in the U.S. since 1973, in some parts of the country it is still imperiling birds like the peregrine falcon and our national symbol, the bald eagle. Because of the residual effects of DDT and a related insecticide called dicofol, some females produce eggs with shells so delicate and thin that they break before viable chicks can hatch.

Oftentimes, you don't even need pesticides, organic or otherwise, to protect food crops. If you catch pest invasions early, you can eliminate the need for pesticides by handpicking or hosing off plants. Check your crops at least once a day—preferably twice—giving special attention to the undersides of leaves where pests prefer to congregate, feed and lay their eggs. Most of them—including cucumber beetles, stink bugs, potato beetles, tomato and tobacco hornworms, cabbageworms, cabbage loopers, scales and Japanese beetles—can be picked off or knocked into a jar of soapy water. Aphids can be hosed off. While hosing doesn't kill them, it gets them off the plant and generally ruins their day. There are stronger measures for dealing with aphids, which are discussed in the following section.

Natural Predators — The Beneficials

Usually, if you let nature take its course, predator insects will help keep populations of destructive pests in check. When aphids appear, ladybird beetles, also called ladybugs, and convergent ladybug larvae are often not far behind. Frankly, though, this is not always an immediate solution. Usually aphid populations must build

Nature provides many insect controls like the aphid-loving ladybird beetles (left), dragonflies (center) and garden spiders (right). Planting a diversity of vegetables, herbs and flowers will help attract such predators.

substantially to attract ladybird beetles and keep them feeding. Even then, they may consume only 70 to 80 percent of the damaging creatures. This is why you need to check your crops thoroughly every day, so you can take an active role in insect control.

Tomato and tobacco hornworms are targeted by a number of birds, especially jays and sparrows. For the last two seasons, we've had a pair of sparrows visit our tomato plants three or four times a day. They hop from branch to branch, looking for worms and keep the plants free of these voracious pests, without hurting the ripening fruit.

Braconid wasps parasitize hornworms by laying eggs under the worms' skin. The developing wasp larvae consume the worm from the inside out. As repugnant as this may sound, better the hornworm than your tomato crop.

Another parasitic wasp, the tiny trichogramma (it has a wingspan of about ⅟₅₀ of an inch), lays its eggs in the eggs of dozens of pests. The larvae devour the pest eggs before they hatch.

Common garden spiders, such as the orb weaver, do a marvelous job of keeping flying pests under control. Many people are afraid of spiders,

but the fact is—with the exceptions of the notorious black widow and brown recluse—spiders are generally harmless to people and are really allies in our battle against destructive pests. Even so, walking into a spider's web can make the most macho man do the comic "spider dance," which looks like a sudden seizure, complete with flailing arms.

Dragonflies and their relatives, the damselflies, should always be a welcome sight in the garden. As they zip around in the air, they draw their legs together to form a "basket" in which they capture flying insects. They then consume their captives on the wing.

Praying mantids (commonly called mantises) sit patiently on a plant with their formidable forelegs drawn up in front of them as if they were praying. When an insect passes by, they quickly finish "saying grace" and seize the luckless creature, devouring it in a trice.

Even yellow jackets, which sometimes show up as party crashers at backyard barbecues, are helpful in the garden. Unlike their smaller relatives, the little wasps that parasitize caterpillars, yellow jackets eat caterpillars. They are particularly fond of imported cabbageworms and cabbage loopers. Yellow

45

jackets can be aggressive to gardeners, too, and will deliver a painful sting if disturbed. So appreciate their good work from a safe distance.

Finally, encourage the best of all the natural predators to visit your garden—birds. Birds sometimes become pests themselves, consuming or damaging fruit and produce, but this is, in our view, balanced out by their insect-control work. Usually, if ripe fruit and produce are harvested or protected by netting, crop losses to birds are reduced to a minimum. Encourage birds to visit by keeping a feeder stocked with a varied selection of bird seed.

Natural Pest Controls

Just as there are natural predators, there are also natural pesticides that are effective, to varying degrees, in controlling destructive insects. Unfortunately, the word "natural" is being misused by those who recognize its profit potential. The traditional meaning, the one we intend, is anything that occurs naturally, from *microbial, plant* or *animal* sources. Anything synthesized, or added to an organic substance, removes it from the "natural" category.

When you use organics, you won't always see the fast knock-down or the sustained control of insects that chemical pesticides deliver. You often must repeat treatments since many organics have a brief life. Some lose their effectiveness quickly in sunlight. But the benefits of growing nontoxic produce are, in our view, well worth any drawbacks of organic pest control. In a world fast becoming overdosed with persistent and lethal chemical poisons, we must be willing to accept something less than perfection in the crops we harvest.

BACILLUS THURINGIENSIS. This is a naturally occurring soil bacterium, often referred to as BT. When insects ingest the material, their digestive system is paralyzed and they eventually die. Several strains of BT have been isolated. The most widely used is called BT *kurstaki*, or BTK. It is toxic to many larvae and caterpillars. BT *san diego* is effective against the larval stage of the Colorado potato beetle. And the strain BT *israelensis* is used against mosquito and black fly larvae. BT strains are available as a dust, as granules and as a liquid. BT is rated as harmless to humans and other mammals. Follow label directions for application methods, timing and frequency. Commercial products include Caterpillar Attack, Caterpillar Killer, Dipel and Thuricide.

Effective against: Cabbage loopers, cabbageworms, codling moth larvae, hornworms, several caterpillars that damage ornamentals and beetle, black fly and mosquito larvae.

Cautions: Pests may build up a resistance to BT, so don't overuse it. Alternate with other controls.

DIATOMACEOUS EARTH (DE). This natural substance is composed of the abrasive silica shells of tiny phytoplankton called diatoms. The sharp extensions of the shells can pierce an insect's body, causing it to "bleed" to death. DE can also absorb wax or oil from an insect's outer coating, causing the creature to become dehydrated. It is available in dust form. Apply when foliage is wet for good adhesion. It can also be applied around the base of plants and watered into the soil to control pests in the root zone. Perma-Guard is a popular commercial product.

Effective against: Aphids, caterpillars, leafhoppers, thrips, slugs, snails and many other soft-bodied pests.

Cautions: Although rated harmless to man and other mammals, inhalation of DE can irritate mucous membranes. Be on the safe side and wear a mask when you handle the material. It is harmful to some beneficial insects, so follow directions for proper use. Use only natural-grade DE.

GARLIC OIL SPRAY. Garlic juice mixed with pure soap and mineral oil is effective against quite a few sap-sucking and leaf-chewing insects. To make this insecticide, finely chop 4 cloves of garlic. Combine with 1 tablespoon of mineral oil, and let stand overnight. Then add 2 cups of water and stir in 1 teaspoon of dish soap (not detergent) free of scents or other additives. Mix thoroughly, then strain the mixture into a container. This makes a concentrate. Dilute 2 tablespoons in 1 pint of lukewarm water to make a spray.

Effective against: Aphids, cabbage loopers, cabbageworms, leafhoppers, mealybugs and whiteflies. It is marginally effective against some leaf-chewers.

Cautions: This control is harmful to most beneficials, so try to avoid spraying when ladybird beetles and other predators are around. Some plants

Insecticidal soaps can be used against aphids and other soft-bodied insects. They have no residual toxic effect.

may be injured by the mixture. Test on a few leaves and watch for results before spraying the entire plant.

INSECTICIDAL SOAPS. Made from fatty acids that are produced naturally by plants and animals, these easily biodegradable substances are effective against a number of soft-bodied sucking insects.

However, their control of chewing pests is limited. They penetrate the insect's body, destroying membranes, and accumulate in their nervous systems, leading to paralysis and death. Unlike most chemical pesticides, they break down quickly, leaving no residual toxic material. They pose no danger to humans and other mammals. Apply at the first sign of infestation and repeat weekly for a month, or until control is gained. Some good commercial products include Safer Fruit & Vegetable Insect Killer, Safer Insecticidal Soap and Savona.

Unfortunately, commercial products are a bit pricey so, before you buy one of them, try mixing your own soap spray from products you may already have around the house. You can use any soap (never detergent) that is pure—free of scents, bleaches and other additives that can damage plant tissue. Both Ivory bar soap and Ivory Liquid Soap are good choices. Start with 1 tablespoon of soap to 1 gallon of warm water. You can enhance the effectiveness of homemade soap sprays by adding either rotenone or pyrethrin to the mix. Increase the strength of the mixture if using the diluted solution seems ineffective.

Effective against: Most soft-bodied pests—aphids, fleas, mealybugs, mites, pear slugs, scales and thrips.

Cautions: Since soaps also kill honeybees, spray early in the morning before bees begin their pollen-collecting rounds. Soaps may damage thin-leaved plants, so test the mix on one leaf before using it on the entire plant.

NICOTINE. This deadly poisonous alkaloid is produced in varying potencies by tobacco plants. It is available as a dust and was formerly sold in concentrated liquid form (nicotine sulfate).

You can make your own nicotine spray by steeping the contents of 2 packages of cigarettes in 1 gallon of hot water, to which you add ½ teaspoon of liquid dish soap. After an hour, strain the decoction through an old nylon stocking or cheesecloth. Leftover spray retains its potency for months if kept in a jar with a screw-top lid. Be sure to label the contents on the container. Commercial products are available; one is called Bonide Tobacco Dust.

Effective against: Most sucking pests that feed on foliage.

Cautions: This spray is toxic to humans and other mammals. It can be absorbed through the skin, through eye tissue and by breathing in sprays. Wear gloves, a respirator and protective eyewear when mixing or spraying. Use on crop plants only up to 30 days before harvest. It is suspected of transmitting tobacco mosaic, so don't use on susceptible plants, such as eggplants, peppers, potatoes and tomatoes.

OIL SPRAYS (DORMANT/SUMMER). Horticultural oils have been improved by removing most of the impurities in the petroleum base, so they can now be used throughout the season to control orchard pests. At one time, they were safe only as dormant oil sprays (to be used only when fruit trees were leafless), because the heavy oil can kill foliage. New oils are lighter, purer and more versatile. They are sometimes referred to as summer, superior or supreme oils, but they may retain their old trade name. They work by coating and smothering insects and their eggs. Refined horticultural oils can be used as a dormant spray to control overwintering insects on fruit trees and as a summer spray to kill new invasions of pests. Diluted oils can also be used on some vegetables. Commercial products include SunSpray Ultra Fine Oil and Volck Oil Spray.

Effective against: Most sucking and chewing insects, their larvae and eggs.

Cautions: Discuss proposed use with your nurseryman. Some plants, especially citrus, may be harmed by oils. Follow label precautions and instructions. It is best used in early morning.

PYRETHRIN. This is a botanical insecticide made from the dried flowers of *Chrysanthemum cinerariifolium.* It is a quick-acting but short-lived poison that is often combined with other insecticides or fungicides to produce a product that offers

Pyrethrin is a nerve poison effective against numerous chewing and sucking insects.

both fast and sustained control or for dealing with two problems at once. Pyrethrin is a nerve poison effective against numerous chewing and sucking insects that attack food crops and ornamentals. Commercial products include Red Arrow and Safer Yard & Garden Insect Killer.

Effective against: Aphids, cabbage loopers, cabbageworms, Colorado potato beetles, leafhoppers, Mexican bean beetles, mites, stink bugs, thrips and whiteflies. It may provide some protection against other pests.

Cautions: Pyrethrin has been shown to kill ladybird beetles and are somewhat toxic to mammals. Hay-fever sufferers may experience an allergic reaction to pyrethrins. Follow label directions carefully for use.

ROTENONE. Often called derris, rotenone is a natural insecticide derived from tropical plants (derris, cubé barbasco and others). It acts as a stomach and contact poison and is best used when mixed with pyrethrin and ryania. This combination does an excellent job of protecting crops and ornamentals against chewing insects (although its potency is short-lived in hot, sunny weather) and is marginally effective in controlling some sucking pests. It is available as a dust, wettable powder or concentrate. Deritox is a widely used commercial brand.

Effective against: Colorado potato beetles, cucumber beetles, flea beetles, Japanese beetles, Mexican bean beetles, scales and tarnished plant bugs.

Cautions: Use the same precautions for protecting against inhalation and skin contact as recommended for nicotine substances. It has proven to be deadly to beneficial insects, birds and aquatic life, somewhat harmful to most domesticated animals and potentially harmful to sensitive humans

Insects that try to cross the Tanglefoot barrier become trapped in the sticky goo.

if inhaled or absorbed through the skin. Even so, it is still safer that many synthetic pesticides on the market.

RYANIA. Extracted from the shrub *Ryania speciosa,* this powerful botanical knocks down a number of chewing and sucking garden pests. It can be used as a spray or dust.

Effective against: Aphids, codling moths, Colorado potato beetles, corn borers, earworms, citrus thrips, Japanese beetles, Mexican bean beetles and squash bugs.

Cautions: Use the same protective measures as noted for mixing and applying nicotine. Follow label instructions for timing and application. Don't use within five to six weeks of harvest or around ponds because of the danger to aquatic life.

SABADILLA. This is another poisonous alkaloid that is effective against a wide range of garden pests. It is extracted from the seeds of a South American member of the lily family. Begin spraying or dusting at the first sign of pests. Two commercial sabadilla products are Necessary Organics Sabadilla Pest Control and Veratran D.

Effective against: Aphids, cabbageworms, cabbage loopers, cucumber beetles, flea beetles, leafhoppers, stink bugs, tarnished plant bugs and thrips.

Cautions: Although not as toxic as nicotine-based extractions, it still should be handled responsibly. It kills bees but is comparatively harmless to other beneficials. Stores well in a dry, dark atmosphere. Follow label guidelines for use.

STICKY BARRIERS. For years, gardeners and orchardists have used Tanglefoot, a nontoxic tacky substance made with castor oil, natural gum resins and vegetable wax to keep chewers and borers out of trees and shrubs. Insects that try to pass through the barrier become trapped in the sticky goo. The best way to use Tanglefoot on fruit trees is to cut a 2-inch-wide piece from a paper towel or toilet paper roll, slit it and wrap it tightly around the trunk a few inches above the soil line. Secure the ends with masking tape. Then, coat the ring with Tanglefoot. Applying the product directly to the trunk can injure the thin bark of fruit trees and may cause girdling.

Effective against: Beetles, caterpillars and other crawling pests.

Cautions: Store containers of Tanglefoot out of reach of children.

STICKY BOARDS. Studies have shown that many flying pests are attracted to the colors yellow and white. This led to the marketing of boards of yellow and white plastic and cardboard, coated with a tacky substance to trap insects. You can make your own sticky boards by painting tongue depressors or pieces of lath bright yellow or white, then coating the top three-quarters with Tanglefoot or Tangle-Trap. Push them into the soil, leaving the sticky part above the surface. There are also commercial sticky traps for catching a number of different flying pests. These include traps for adult moths of corn earworms, cabbage loopers and peach tree borers and for cherry fruit flies. In addition, there are sticky traps that include a scent lure (pheromone) to attract males looking for a mate. One attracts codling moths, another draws Japanese beetles. We feel the scent lures are not that great an idea (See Home Remedies & Myths, page 62).

Effective against: Yellow boards attract aphids, black flies, gnats, leafhoppers, moths and whiteflies; white boards lure tarnished plant bugs and flea beetles.

Cautions: Store containers of Tanglefoot and Tangle-Trap out of reach of children.

TENTING. There are several kinds of row covers and netting you can use to protect your crops from flying insects and caterpillar-producing moths. Two we like are the lightweight, tightly woven pest netting and the equally lightweight polypropylene fabric barrier. Both are priced at about $7 for pieces 6 feet by 16 feet. They can be draped over stakes or cages to prevent pests from landing on foliage. There is only a slight heat buildup under the polypropylene fabric. Both admit light and moisture and, with care, can be used for several seasons.

Effective against: Most flying pests.

Cautions: For crops that need to be pollinated, remove the cover in late morning when bees are active, then replace it. Watch for wilting heat-sensitive crops like lettuce.

A Rogue's Gallery of Garden Pests

The following roster of garden pests is not intended to be a complete encyclopedia of insects that feed on and damage crop plants. It is as complete a list as we can make of pests you may encounter in container farming. By growing plants in pots, you don't have to deal with a number of soil-dwelling pests, such as beetles, nematodes, cutworms and other grubs. Even some of the crawlers and creepers, like snails and slugs, aren't much of a problem in the container garden, since there are fewer places for them to hide.

If you do notice a critter not described in the following section, there are a number of reference books (see Selected Publications, page 122) you can refer to for identification. One of the best is the *Organic Gardener's Handbook of Natural Insect and Disease Control.*

ANTS. These have the reputation of being a gardener's friend because they clean up dead insects. But in our view, the ant is one of the worst garden pests, and we are only glad it's not a larger insect. While it is true that ants themselves seldom feed on plants, they spread other insect damagers from infested crops to healthy ones. Aphids, mealybugs and soft scales all excrete a sweet, sticky substance called honeydew that ants consider *haute cuisine.* In fact, some ants subsist almost exclusively on honeydew. To increase production of honeydew, which they coax from insects by stroking them, ants "farm" honeydew producers, especially aphids. They move the pests from plant to plant to establish new colonies. Honeydew is also a prime food source for sooty mold fungus, which can turn leaves and branches black as it spreads, blocking light and transpiration. If you see ants traveling up and down

| *Aphids* | *Cabbage Looper* | *Corn Earworm* |

plant stems or tree trunks, you can be sure you have an infestation of sap-sucking insects.

Controls: To control ants, rid your plants of their honeydew producers or use ant stakes and sticky barriers around stems and trunks. Although there are ant pesticides, we don't recommend them, especially around food crops.

To discourage ants from nesting in your containers or farming aphids on your plants, we suggest using black, red or chili pepper. Apply in bands or sprinkle around plants. Boric acid is also effective in controlling ant invasions. It acts as a stomach poison. Mix 3 tablespoons of boric acid with 1 teaspoon of sugar and sprinkle liberally around plants where ants are a problem.

APHIDS. In addition to weakening and sometimes destroying plants by sucking the life out of them, aphids are also one of the worst vectors of plant diseases. They inject viruses as they feed. Aphids come in an array of colors—white, yellow, green, brown, black and pink. Another type, the woolly aphid, resembles the mealybug. When an aphid population can no longer be sustained by a given food source, females called "stem mothers" give birth to winged young, which fly off to colonize another plant. Aphids have several natural predators. Chief among them are ladybird beetles and their larvae, aphid lions (green lacewings), hover fly larvae and predatory braconid wasps.

Controls: First, try hosing aphids off plants with a sharp spray of water. This won't kill them, but it will disrupt their feeding. Once hosed off, they probably won't return to the host plant. For heavy infestations, spray plants with Safer Fruit & Vegetable Insect Killer or use pyrethrin or rotenone.

CABBAGE LOOPERS. These light green caterpillars with a white stripe along each side are common destructive larvae of a small brown moth. Moths usually appear when the weather heats up to lay eggs on cole crops (such as cabbage and collards). Loopers also feed on celery, lettuce, peas and spinach. Their common name comes from their "looping" action (similar to the movement of inchworms) as they travel. They feed on leaves and stems, and unchecked, they can ravage whole crops.

Controls: BT *(Bacillus thuringiensis)* applied weekly in early spring will usually prevent looper damage. Other effective treatments include garlic sprays, pyrethrin and sabadilla. If you're not squeamish, you can also pick caterpillars off by hand. Loopers also have natural enemies—*Apanteles glomeratus* and chalcid wasps.

CODLING MOTHS. Larvae of the codling moth ruin more apples than any other pest. Adult moths appear in May, when most fruit trees are in full bloom. They are grayish brown with a wingspan of about ¾ inch. Their forewings have white lines across them and their hindwings are tan to brown. They lay their flat eggs on fruit, foliage and branches. Ten to fourteen days later, pinkish white caterpillars with brown heads emerge. They bore their way into fruit, tunneling into the center. Their presence is apparent from their waste—a brownish, crumbly substance around the entry hole. Targeted fruits include apple, apricot, cherry, peach, pear and plum.

Controls: Use pheromone traps in early spring if codling moths have been a problem in the past. Once moths begin to appear in traps, release trichogramma wasps to parasitize eggs. After most of the flower petals have dropped, spray trees with ryania and repeat at one-week intervals three more times. Use sticky barriers on trunks close to the ground to trap larvae.

COLORADO POTATO BEETLES. Both adult beetles and larvae are destructive to a number of vegetable crops—eggplants, peppers, tomatoes and potatoes among them. Beetles are less than ½ inch long, orange and yellow, with ten bold black stripes running lengthwise on their wing covers. Larvae are orange, plump and decorated with black spots running the length of their bodies.

Controls: You can handpick beetles and drop them into a jar of hot, soapy water. If you aren't enamored of this technique, you can spray weekly applications of pyrethrin, rotenone or the *san diego* strain of BT. Predators that can help you control

potato bugs are ladybird beetles, spiders and tachinid flies and wasps.

CORN EARWORMS. Also called the tomato fruitworm, this pest ravages many crops, including tomatoes, beans, broccoli, cabbage and lettuce, but its favorite target is tender, developing ears of sweet corn. It feeds on kernels and leaves a repulsive trail of excrement. It may prevent silk pollination by consuming tassels, which produce pollen. Like hornworms, earworms also devour tomato foliage, but unlike hornworms, they tunnel through the fruit, ruining it for harvest. Adults are dusky brown moths about 1½ inches wide. Female moths lay eggs by the hundreds on host plants. Eggs are laid along corn silks and the hatched larvae then begin eating their way down into the ears.

Earworms may be yellow, green, pink or dark brown and all have dark and light stripes. Emerging larvae are white with black heads.

Controls: Ryania and BT (strain *kurstaki*) are effective against earworms. Parasitic wasps prey on them.

CUCUMBER BEETLES (SPOTTED/STRIPED). This extremely prolific and destructive pest attacks a number of vining crop plants. It chews on stems, leaves and fruit, spreads bacterial wilt and mosaic disease and produces larvae that feed on plant roots (spotted beetle larvae on corn roots, striped beetle larvae on squash). Striped beetles are about ¼ inch

Spotted/Striped Cucumber Beetles

Tobacco Hornworm

Imported Cabbageworm

long and have yellow wing covers with three black stripes and black heads. Spotted varieties are the same size and color but have 11 black spots on their wings.

Controls: Adults can be checked with pyrethrin, rotenone or sabadilla sprays. Larvae of both can be virtually eliminated with weekly applications of parasitic nematodes into the soil around the root zone.

FLEA BEETLES. There are several kinds of flea beetles, each named after the plant it feeds on—corn, eggplant, grape, spinach and strawberry. All are less than ¼ inch long but vary in color, ranging from black to dark blue and metallic brass to greenish black. Adults leap around like fleas when disturbed. Most lay eggs around a plant's base. Small, white grubs hatch from these eggs and burrow down to feed on roots and tubers. They then pupate and emerge as adults about two weeks later. Adults feed on upper leaf surfaces, riddling the foliage with holes. Seedlings are a favorite target.

Controls: To control soil-borne larvae, drench soil with parasitic nematodes. At the first sign of leaf damage, spray plants with pyrethrin, rotenone or sabadilla.

HORNWORMS (TOBACCO/TOMATO). Although differing slightly in markings, both hornworms are equally destructive to tomato plants. The tobacco hornworm has a red horn on its tail with seven diagonal stripes of white on its sides. The tomato hornworm's horn is black and has eight white stripes. Either can quickly defoliate a plant, leaving only stem and fruit. Young plants often die. Fruits on older plants won't mature normally and are susceptible to sunburn from the loss of protective foliage. Look for black droppings on leaves—evidence that a hornworm, cleverly disguised to resemble a curled tomato leaf, is feeding on the underside of a leaf above.

Controls: The easiest method of dealing with hornworms is to pick them off with a gloved hand and drop them into a container of hot, soapy water. In lieu of this, sprinkle tomato plants with BT powder (strain *kurstaki*). Braconid wasps are natural enemies of hornworms. They parasitize them by laying their eggs inside the worms so their offspring will have a ready source of food. Since tomato plants are self-fertile and need no insects to pollinate them, you can cover plants with lightweight nylon netting draped over cages to keep adult moths from laying eggs in the foliage.

IMPORTED CABBAGEWORMS. Another destroyer of cole crops, these larvae of a prevalent white butterfly are velvety and light green and seem to have a particular affinity for collards and broccoli. However, they can also destroy the vegetable they're named for in short order. As quickly as you rid your crops of them, another butterfly appears to plague you with a new generation. This continues until either the harvest or the onset of cool weather.

Controls: Usually, covering cole crops with fine netting, held up with tomato stakes, will block the butterflies' access to the plants. You can also spray weekly with BT (strain *kurstaki*) or every two weeks with sabadilla. Wasps (especially yellow jackets) will help you control these larvae.

JAPANESE BEETLES. Adult beetles have a sinister beauty. Their bodies are a glossy green and their wing covers a coppery orange. These ½-inch-long piranhas of the insect kingdom congregate into an eating machine of hundreds to consume foliage on plum and other fruit trees. They devour from the bottom to the topmost leaf, leaving only a denuded skeleton before moving on to their next victim. They also produce legions of white grubs with light brown heads that feed on roots, usually of turf grasses. Japanese beetles have an omnivorous appetite and damage a wide range of food crops and ornamentals.

Controls: It is doubtful that Japanese beetles or their grubs pose much of a problem in the container garden. But, if you see beetles on your trees or crops, go to work before they do. Pick them off and drown them in soapy water, or spray infested plants with rotenone. There are Japanese beetle traps that do an excellent job of attracting and then trapping beetles. They consist of a plastic hanger with a bag underneath. On the hanger, you place a self-adhesive strip of a pheromone, or sex attractant, as bait. The beetles bump against the bait and slide down

| Japanese Beetles | Leaf Miners | Mealybugs |

into the bag, where they are trapped. We're not big fans of sex traps because they seem to bring more beetles into an area than would be present without them. (See Home Remedies & Myths, page 62.)

LEAFHOPPERS. For their small size (¹⁄₁₆ inch to ½ inch long), leafhoppers do an awful lot of damage. But of the more than 2,000 species of leafhoppers, only a few are garden pests. The most common is the light green potato hopper, which is wedge-shaped and carries its wings high over its body. These insects suck sap from foliage and stems and often damage or kill such plants as beans, celery, eggplant, peanuts, potatoes and apple and citrus trees. They also inject toxic saliva as they feed, transmitting virus diseases that are usually the death knell for weakened plants. The pale green to brown beet hopper is prevalent in the western states. It transmits the viruses curly top and yellows in tomatoes. Symptoms are overall yellowing of foliage and some distortion in leaves, which may also have warty veins and overall weak, stunted growth. When disturbed, some hoppers move rapidly sideways like crabs or leap into the air. Adults will usually fly out of harm's way. The nymphs are pale and wingless and hop acrobatically if approached.

Controls: Spray infested plants with insecticidal soap, pyrethrin, rotenone or sabadilla. Natural enemies include predatory flies and wasps.

LEAF MINERS. This name is given to the larvae of several insects that tunnel between the leaf layers of a number of vegetable and ornamental plants. The appearance of their serpentine, or sometimes round, "mines" on leaves is often the first indication that you have a leaf miner problem. Look for clusters of tiny, round white eggs stuck to the undersides of leaves. Scrape these off and destroy them. Plants are severely weakened by the mining activity of these pests, and this often affects fruit production or causes deformities.

Controls: Snip off mined leaves and discard them in the rubbish bin.

MEALYBUGS. These are common pests in both southern and central areas, but they may also be an occasional nuisance in northern gardens. Adults are about the size of a match head. They have pink, segmented bodies coated with filaments of white, cottony fluff, which is a protective wax secreted to form a shield against the desiccating effects of the sun. It also protects them somewhat from pesticides. The adults and nymphs, which are pale yellow, are equally efficient at extracting sap. This weakens and reduces the productivity of plants. Mealybugs also excrete honeydew, which attracts ants to feed on the sugary substance. Mealybugs congregate in several generations on plants, usually in crotches, on fruit stems and at leaf nodes.

Controls: A sharp jet of water will usually dislodge colonies, or you can spray them with insecticidal soap. Another approach is to use a cotton swab to apply a solution of 10 percent rubbing alcohol and 90 percent water directly to the mealybugs and to leaf nodes and other parts of plants where they congregate. The alcohol solution is not harmful to plants and can even be applied to African violets without hurting the foliage. Natural enemies include the fierce mealybug destroyer *Cryptolaemus montrouzieri* and its larvae and the parasitic wasp *Leptomastix dactylopii.*

MEXICAN BEAN BEETLE. This relative of the beneficial ladybird beetle has none of its good qualities. Adults are about the same size as ladybugs, but they are coppery brown and have 16 black spots on their wing covers as opposed to a ladybird's 12. Adults and their larvae are equally destructive to bean crops, feeding on pods and stems and eating lacy patterns in leaves. Their eggs are oval and are deposited on end, on the undersides of leaves. Each female is capable of laying up to 500 eggs each season; eggs hatch in less than two weeks into orangish grubs studded with forked spines.

Controls: Weekly sprayings of pyrethrin, rotenone or sabadilla are usually effective in controlling this pest. Look under foliage for eggs and destroy any that you find. Both parasitic wasps and spined soldier bugs are natural enemies of Mexican bean beetles.

MITES. Of the hundreds of species of mites, there are two that can cause problems with food crops—the rust mite and the spider mite. Both of them feed on the leaves of fruit and vegetables. These almost microscopic pests damage plants by drawing out vital sap with their stylets. The damage is usually not noticed until a large colony has established itself on a plant victim. The feeding activity of rust mites gives both foliage and fruit a russet appearance. Spider mite activity causes leaves to take on a dull, yellowish, speckled appearance and often promotes early fruit drop. Occasionally, these distant relatives of spiders spin incomplete webs or strands of webbing, which is another clue to their presence.

Controls: Rust mites can be controlled with a sulfur fungicide applied to the foliage. Dormant trees should be sprayed with a horticultural oil containing lime sulfur. Spider mites on vegetables and berries can be eradicated with insecticidal soap, pyrethrin or rotenone. On fruit trees, release predatory mites *(Metaseiulus occidentalis).*

PEAR SAWFLYS. Adults appear in early spring to early summer to saw slits in leaves and deposit tiny flattened eggs into these openings. In about a week, yellowish slug-like larvae hatch and immediately begin to feed on upper leaf surfaces of cherry, pear and plum trees, leaving only a network of veins and necrotic tissue. As they mature, larvae excrete slime and turn a dull green. A second invasion usually occurs in late summer, sometimes as late as September. Unchecked infestations can defoliate trees.

Controls: At the first sign of infestation, spray trees with pyrethrin or rotenone. Follow with another application in a week. Watch for a second wave after July.

PEPPER WEEVILS. These small ⅛-inch-long pests are brownish red or black, have a curved snout and are very similar in appearance to curculios. They feed on fruit and lay eggs inside it that hatch into tiny, maggot-like grubs. The larvae also eat the fruit and pupate into adults, after which they join other adult weevils outside, where they continue to ravage peppers. You'll first notice tiny puncture holes encircled by brown or black rings.

Controls: Infested fruit should be removed and destroyed. Then, spray plants with rotenone.

SCALES (SOFT/ARMORED). Scale insects are not much of a pest on herbaceous (soft-tissue) plants but are a real nuisance on dwarf fruit trees or berries (cane fruit and bush types). Scales damage plants by both feeding on sap and injecting toxic saliva into their host. Most types also excrete honeydew, which attracts ants to feed on it. If honeydew production is heavy, sooty mold fungus may develop, which further endangers the health of the tree.

Hard-shelled (armored) scales protect themselves by secreting a coating of wax-like fibers, often layering one coat upon another. This substance hardens into a thick "shell" that is impervious to pesticides. Soft scales have a similar protective cov-

Pepper Weevils   *San Jose Scale*   *Soft Scale*

ering that is actually part of the insect.

Of the thousands of scale species that feed on crop plants, four have become particular problems for the fruit and berry grower. The two worst armored scales are the oystershell and the San Jose types. Oystershell scales are found in most parts of the country on stone-fruit trees, grapes and raspberries. With their grayish covering, they look like miniature oysters. San Jose scales may be either gray or brown. They appear as tiny nodules on branches. They can quickly cover a branch, posing a serious threat to the branch's well-being.

Two of the peskiest soft scales are the cottony cushion scale and the European fruit lecanium. The former are more noticeable because of their egg masses, which resemble small wads of cotton. They pose a threat to citrus trees, but European fruit lecaniums are probably more prevalent on all types of fruit trees. They are brown, shiny and smaller than the head of a match.

Controls: Because of their protective shells, scale insects are generally unaffected by sprays. Once they've formed their hardened skin, they don't move again but attach themselves permanently to a feeding spot. We've found that the most successful method of dealing with scale insects is to scrape them off with a thumbnail or metal nail file, then spray the branch with pyrethrin or rotenone to kill exposed eggs and nymphs.

SLUGS & SNAILS. These destructive pests, which are relatives of clams and mollusks, can decimate a container of seedlings overnight. They are a serious garden pest in warm and humid areas of the country but less so in other regions. They come in a number of colors, brown being the most common. Slugs look like fat, slimy worms with two prong-like antennae on their heads. Snails are similar in color but carry a mottled shell into which they retreat when disturbed. Both are imperiled by the dehydrating effects of the sun, so they usually feed at night and on overcast days.

They hide under foliage, mulch, containers, boards or garden debris during the heat of the day. They chew their way through the stems, leaves and fruit of almost all crop plants, completely devouring tender plants and seedlings. Damaged fruit can often be salvaged by cutting away the portion on which the pests were feeding.

Controls: We advocate handpicking and destroying these pests. There are pellets and meals that are popular with some gardeners, but we consider these too dangerous, especially around food crops. A good natural control is diatomaceous earth, which is composed of the razor-sharp silica shells of tiny phytoplankton called diatoms. It is rated harmless to humans and pets. Sprinkle rings of DE around the base of plants if snail infestations are severe.

SQUASH VINE BORERS. These are more of a

problem in the eastern than the western half of the country. Adults are colorful moths about an inch long with red abdomens accented with black. The female appears about the time vine crops are getting established and lays one tiny reddish brown egg at a time. These hatch about seven to ten days later into white grubs with brown heads that immediately begin boring into stems and vines of cucumbers, gourds, melons, pumpkins and squash. As they eat the soft interior of the stem, they cause the plant to wilt and often die. Look for yellow to light brown excrement on the topsoil under vines.

Controls: If you catch infestations early, before larvae have tunneled into vines, you can gain the upper hand by spraying plants with rotenone. If you're too late to catch the larvae before they've entered the vines, you can slit open the infested section, dig out and destroy the larvae, then bury that section and the closest stem joint under a pile of soil. This may promote rooting at the stem joint and regenerate the plant.

STINK BUGS. These earned their common name from their habit of exuding a fluid with an offensive odor whenever they're disturbed. Both adults and nymphs draw out sap from host plants: fruits, vegetables and ornamentals. Fruits and tomatoes are often ruined in appearance and rendered unappealing by this feeding activity. Stink bugs are shaped like a shield, and one—the harle-

quin bug—is brightly colored with orange or yellow markings on its black body. It is a major pest of cole crops, especially in the South.

Controls: Check the undersides of leaves weekly for clusters of the unique, barrel-shaped egg masses. Dust plants with sabadilla or spray with pyrethrin. A natural predator of stink bugs is the tachinid fly.

THRIPS. These are not as common a garden pest as aphids and caterpillar larvae, but they are equally destructive in large numbers. A fraction of an inch long, these yellowish white to brownish black critters and their nymphs tear the foliage and drink the sap that oozes from the wounds, causing yellowing and weakening of the plant. You'll notice silver streaking on foliage where thrips are feeding. Populations mushroom in late summer, so early control is imperative.

Controls: Before leaf-out and after the growing season, spray dormant oil on fruit trees. Yellow sticky traps attract and capture flying adults. When fruit begins to form, spray trees with pyrethrin or insecticidal soap. On vegetable crops, spray ryania or dust leaves with sabadilla or diatomaceous earth.

WHITEFLIES. The almost microscopic whitefly, which resembles a tiny moth, is a fast-multiplying pest that sucks sap from the undersides of leaves of a broad range of edible and ornamental plants. When disturbed, colonies rise up in a cloud. One female can produce 300 eggs in a month. Both

Slug & Brown Snail

Whiteflies

Whitefly Sticky Trap

adults and nymphs feed on plants and often inject hosts with virus diseases.

Controls: One of the best weapons against whiteflies is a yellow sticky trap, which these flies find irresistible. Spray heavily infested plants with insecticidal soap, garlic oil, pyrethrin or rotenone.

Diseases and Their Control

There are three basic types of diseases that infect food crops—fungal, bacterial and viral. Some virus diseases are introduced to plants by insect vectors, or carriers, who pass them on through toxic saliva as they feed. Others are present in a dormant state on seeds or plants and merely wait for the right conditions to develop. Still others are brought on by warm or cool, damp weather that keeps foliage moist and by wind that blows disease-carrying spores. Allowing decaying vegetation to collect in containers and around plants also creates a favorable breeding ground for diseases.

There are some simple steps you can take to prevent fungus diseases from getting a foothold in your container garden. One way is never to let your plants go to bed wet. This means if you use overhead irrigation, do it early enough in the day so that the moisture has time to evaporate from leaf surfaces before the sun goes down.

Another is to avoid working around plants when they're wet. Moisture is a good conductor of plant-disease pathogens. If you prune or handle a diseased plant, even a dry one, wash your hands with soap and dip your pruner blades into a mix of 10 percent alcohol and 90 percent water before working on other plants.

Seeds—especially those collected in the field or saved from home gardens—may be carrying a disease. Even purchased seeds sometimes have hitchhiking pathogens, although this is rare. You can sterilize suspect seeds before planting by dousing them in a 10 percent alcohol solution and drying them on a paper towel. Or, pour seeds into an old cotton sock and suspend them in a pot of hot wa-

ter. Feed a skewer or similar rod through the top of the sock so the seeds are kept off the bottom of the pot. Use a candy thermometer to check the temperature. Most disease pathogens are killed after about 25 minutes at 122 degrees F. Once the seeds have been heat-sterilized, they should be sown immediately, since this treatment stimulates germination.

Container-grown plants purchased at local nurseries, especially berries, should be checked for evidence of viral disease. Look for limp, blackened or off-color foliage or a general lack of vigor. Most long-established mail-order nurseries ship plants that are guaranteed to be free of disease.

Finally, keep fallen leaves and fruit picked out of containers so that you don't provide a breeding place for diseases or a hiding spot for destructive insects. If vegetation or fruit has a disease, consign it to the rubbish bin, not your compost pile.

Funguses

ANTHRACNOSE. The first evidence of this fungus is on the leaves. Small yellow spots of dead tissue appear, then expand and turn brown or black. Decaying tissue eventually falls out to leave irregular holes. Fruit develops dark, sunken lesions. Damp weather causes diseases to spread rapidly.

Susceptible plants: Beans, cucumbers, melons, peas, peppers, tomatoes and watermelons.

Controls: Shop for anthracnose-resistant varieties. Clean up fallen debris. If disease appears, prune off affected foliage, sterilize pruning tools, then spray with a fungicide to halt the spread.

BLACK ROT. On vegetable crops, the disease begins as irregular light yellowish spots on foliage that soon turn black. Other forms of rot may follow. On cabbage, yellowish brown wedges appear on leaf margins. Grapes shrivel into hard, raisin-like "mummies." Their foliage becomes flecked with black and brown spots. Flesh of certain vine crops may rot.

Susceptible plants: Cabbages, cucumbers, grapes, pumpkins, sweet potatoes, turnips and winter squash.

Black Rot

Damping-Off Disease

Downy Mildew

Controls: You may be able to find rot-resistant varieties. Before disease develops on grapes, spray plants with bordeaux mixture or some other copper-based fungicide, before and after blooming. To halt the spread of disease, dispose of any infested plants.

BOTRYTIS BLIGHT. Cool, humid weather and poor air circulation provide the ideal conditions for this destructive fungal disease. Leaves of crop plants first show darkened water-soaked areas that eventually turn brown as tissue dies. Strawberries develop a gray mold that covers and destroys the entire berry.

Susceptible plants: Brambles, cabbage, grapes, onions and strawberries as well as ornamentals and herbaceous plants.

Controls: Your best hope is to halt the spread of the disease. This is done by improving air circulation around plants and pruning out and discarding infected portions.

DAMPING-OFF DISEASE. Most gardeners who have started plants from seed have experienced this disappointing phenomenon at least once or twice. Seedlings are either killed before they ever appear (preemergent form) or keel over from stems that rot at the soil line a few days after they've germinated (postemergent form).

Susceptible plants: All.

Controls: The major causes of damping-off disease are using unsterilized mixes and dirty containers to start seedlings. Overly wet mixes and cool temperatures can contribute to the problem. Make sure excess water drains freely. Using peat moss in the seedling mix and planting in peat containers definitely minimizes the disease, but it does not always prevent it. Never start seeds in just soil. It is usually loaded with dormant disease pathogens, and one of these may be damping-off fungus.

DOWNY MILDEW. This is one of the most commonly encountered fungus diseases in the garden. And, like most fungal disorders, it is usually triggered by spells of wet, humid weather. Initially, you'll notice yellow spots on the upper surface of leaves, while the underside will have a white, tan or purplish downy mold. Eventually, the leaves turn brown as the tissue dies.

Susceptible plants: Cole crops, cucumbers, grapes, lettuce, melons, onions and many other food crops and ornamental plants.

Controls: Seek out fungus-resistant varieties. Apply a preventive spray of bordeaux mix or another copper-based fungicide, which can also be used to halt the progress of the disease.

EARLY/LATE BLIGHT. Both diseases are spread by damp, humid conditions, but the pathogens may be present on purchased or collected plants. Early blight develops initially on lower leaves and moves upward. It begins as brown spots with in-

Fusarium Wilt   *Blossom-End Rot*   *Smut*

ner concentric rings that soon cover the entire leaf. Plants can be defoliated if the disease is not checked. Dark spots and rot may appear on fruit. Late blight symptoms are small, dark spots often accompanied by a grayish white mold on the undersurface of the leaves. Fruit deteriorates and shrivels.

Susceptible plants: Potatoes and tomatoes.

Controls: Buy resistant varieties and certified disease-free seed potatoes. Remove diseased plants and discard.

FUSARIUM WILT. The first symptoms of this disease are often mistaken for dehydration. Leaves curl upward and droop in the heat of the day, then recover after sundown. As the disease advances, yellow patches appear on the leaves and these ultimately turn brown. Often, the lowest foliage is affected first. (The presence of the disease can be confirmed by cutting a stem and inspecting its interior. A brown discoloration indicates fusarium wilt.) Plants in the final stage of the disease wilt and never recover.

Susceptible plants: Peas, peppers, potatoes, tomatoes, vine crops and some ornamentals.

Controls: Plant only fusarium-resistant varieties. Affected plants should be discarded. Don't replant crops in the same mix, since it may harbor wilt disease pathogens.

GRAY MOLD. This disease first appears as dark, water-soaked areas on leaves and stems. Hu-mid weather spurs the development of a gray mold, which is the fruiting body of the disease. If unchecked, the entire plant, including the fruit, will be consumed.

Susceptible plants: Eggplants, lettuce, okra, onions, squash, strawberries and many other herbaceous and ornamental plants.

Controls: Prune off affected portions of the plant and discard in the rubbish bin. Ornamental plants can be sprayed weekly with sulfur to prevent reinfection, which usually occurs during cool, damp weather.

PEACH LEAF CURL. A cool, wet spring provides the ideal conditions for this disease. Leaves are covered with yellow, brown or red blisters (sometimes all three at once) and become distorted. Surfaces take on a grayish, powdery cast. Fruit is equally damaged. Infected leaves and fruit drop as the disease progresses.

Susceptible plants: Peaches and nectarines.

Controls: Plant resistant varieties. A spray of bordeaux mix or lime sulfur, applied while a tree is dormant, may offer some protection. If it rains within two weeks of application, repeat. For infected trees, prune off and discard diseased portions, then spray with sulfur to prevent reinfection. Repeat in damp, humid weather.

SCAB. This disease causes rough, corky, raised spots or depressions on tubers and roots. As the disease progresses, these areas expand. The ailment is largely cosmetic. Affected portions can be peeled off and the rest of the tuber saved.

Susceptible plants: Most root crops, especially beets, potatoes and radishes. There are also fruit scabs that affect apples and pears in particular.

Controls: This disease prospers in alkaline, sandy soils. Keep the mix on the acidic side (below pH 5.5). Don't add manures or wood ashes to the mix.

SMUT. This disease first appears as small green and white gall-like swellings on the ears, leaves, stalks and tassels of corn. When the disease reaches its final stage, the galls turn sooty, then burst open to release hundreds of smut-carrying spores.

Susceptible plants: Sweet corn.

Controls: There are smut-resistant varieties of corn available. Removing infested parts of the plant immediately—especially before galls open—can sometimes curb the disease.

Viruses

CURLY TOP. Plant leaves infected with curly top become distorted, curled and leathery, losing their healthy green appearance quickly. Affected foliage and stems turn yellow then brown. Fruit already formed doesn't mature, and production of new fruit is arrested.

Susceptible plants: Beans, beets, melons, spinach and a number of soft-tissue ornamentals.

Controls: Shop for resistant varieties. Leafhoppers are vectors of curly top. Infected plants usually can't be saved; uproot and discard them.

MOSAIC. These diseases, which affect a large variety of plants, are usually transmitted by aphids and leafhoppers as they feed. The symptoms are greenish or yellowish mottling of leaves, which creates a pattern similar to a mosaic tile design, hence the common name. Fruit develops similar splotches and may appear warty.

Susceptible plants: Beans, cucumbers, corn, lettuce, melons, peppers, spinach, squash and a great many others, including some ornamentals.

Controls: Some resistant varieties are available. Controlling vectors (aphids and leafhoppers) will

help prevent disease. Infected plants are doomed; remove and discard them.

Bacterial Diseases

BACTERIAL BLIGHT. This blight may appear if the weather is wet and humid. Leaves, pods and stems develop water-soaked spots or white growth. Spots brown off and become brittle. Warmer, drier weather sometimes stops the spread of this disease.

Susceptible plants: Beans and peas.

Controls: Prune off diseased portions and spray plants with copper fungicide to help control any reinfection.

BACTERIAL WILT. Symptoms include sudden wilting or dieback of leaves, runners and sometimes the entire plant. Darkened, water-soaked spots may develop on the leaves. Verify the presence of the disease by cutting open a portion of the stem. Strands of a white tacky substance will ooze out if the plant is infected.

Susceptible plants: Particularly cucumbers, melons and squash, but many other vegetables are susceptible too.

Controls: Buy resistant varieties. Control cucumber beetles and grasshoppers, both vectors of bacterial wilt, before they have a chance to transmit the disease. Infected plants are not salvageable; remove and discard them.

Physiological Disorders

BLOSSOM-END ROT. Undoubtedly the most common problem encountered when growing tomatoes, this disorder is caused by erratic watering (allowing the mix to dry out, then irrigating), a calcium deficiency in the mix or both. Fruit develops soft spots on the bottom, or blossom end, that eventually become hard black areas. Although unsightly, they do not render the fruit inedible. Simply cut off affected portions.

Susceptible plants: Eggplants, peppers and tomatoes.

Controls: Keep the soil in containers evenly moist. Mulch heavily with organic matter, plastic or crumpled newspapers. Don't use high-nitrogen fertilizers. Spray plants with a calcium chloride solution if your crop is seriously threatened.

Mycoplasmas

YELLOWS. This condition is transmitted to plants by leafhoppers. Symptoms include yellowing of new foliage and a dwarfing and deforming of the entire plant. Leaves often curl, yellow and drop prematurely. Lettuce plants often bolt (go to seed), and carrots develop hairy roots and occasionally take on a bitter taste.

Susceptible plants: Carrots, lettuce, onions, tomatoes and many ornamentals.

Controls: Eliminate leafhoppers and you will minimize the chances of infection. Plants with yellows can't be saved, although some fruit, such as green tomatoes can be harvested and ripened in a sunny kitchen window.

Home Remedies & Myths

There are probably ten times as many unconventional or homespun cures for garden ills as there are problems, pests and diseases. Many of these are only marginally effective; some create a new problem while solving the original one; a few are merely a waste of time.

Here are some of these bits of lore, followed by our observations. We encourage you to experiment and, ultimately, arrive at your own conclusions.

Snail & slug control. Three of the most frequently encountered methods of dealing with these pesky mollusks are (1) the salt-and-flashlight gambit, (2) the drink-and-drown scenario and (3) the ashes-and-sand-bars method.

The first calls for visiting your garden containers at night with a salt-shaker and flashlight and sprinkling marauding slugs or snails with salt. This will certainly kill the critters, but salt that ends up in the mix probably does more harm to the plants than the invaders do.

The second method is based on the theory that placing saucers of beer around plants lures slugs and snails to their death by attracting them to the brew, which they then drown in. We have yet to hear of anyone having much success with this method—although there may be a lot of pleasantly inebriated and grateful snails in container gardens across America who support it.

Finally, home-grown wisdom says that sprinkling rings of ashes or sand around plants provides a surefire barrier to slugs and snails, since it fouls up the trail of secreted slime on which they travel. This is true—so long as the ashes and sand stay dry. A heavy dew, light rain or irrigating the garden turns these formidable ramparts into minor hindrances. For these barriers to work, you must frequently add fresh, dry sand or ashes.

In our opinion, handpicking is the most sensible solution to snail and slug infestations.

Aphid control. Sprinkling ashes on foliage is touted as a repellent to these little sapsuckers. The problem is, aphids feed on the undersides of leaves, where ashes won't stick. We think a brisk hosing or a shower of insecticidal soap is the best way to contend with aphids.

Ants are useful scavengers. Ants do clean up dead insects, aerate soil and feed on destructive root organisms. But, in our book, they're still a big problem. Because of their addiction to honeydew, the sweet substance (mostly undigested plant sap) excreted by aphids, scales and several other pests, ants spread aphids throughout the garden, tending and protecting them against beneficial insects. Also, they often find the light, loose soil mix in containers irresistible for nesting sites and disturbing roots with their continual tunneling. Ants also invade hummingbird feeders for the nectar. We're glad ants aren't any larger than they are. With their industriousness and strength, they'd rule the garden—maybe the world.

Sex scent traps control flying pests. While it is true that sex scent (pheromone) traps lure a number of destructive pests to their death, we have serious reservations about them. We think the traps lure insects to your garden that otherwise would not have

Traps, such as this sticky-coated sphere for apple maggots, reduce insect damage without noxious fumes.

stopped by. In our view, the only sensible method would be to enroll the entire block or neighborhood in a trapping operation or wait until your garden is actually invaded before installing pheromone traps.

Releasing beneficial insects helps control pests. This one appears to us to fall into the myth category. The idea here—and it has a lot of knowledgeable proponents—is that you buy beneficial insects (either as eggs, larvae, pupae or adults) and release them in your garden. They then consume the insects that feed on and damage your crops. While this appears to be a commendable endeavor, it can be a waste of time and money. First of all, there is no guarantee that the creatures will stay where you want them. If there is no immediate and substantial food source in your container garden, they may fly to your neighbor's garden or some more distant spot.

Consider, too, that those "live predators" you purchase often have been shipped long distances under difficult conditions. Many may be dead on arrival or will die soon after being suddenly released into the hot, sunny environment of your container garden.

One exception, we should note, to the flyaway habit of many beneficials, including ladybird beetles and parasitic wasps, is the green lacewing. If you buy and distribute the eggs of this insect, they will hatch into what are often called "aphid lions." Gen-erally, they will stay put long enough to consume whole colonies of aphids. Some of our gardening friends report satisfactory results from these and other beneficials. Certainly, an increasing number of gardeners are buying them from mail-order firms (see Sources, page 120) and some nurseries. However, we have not had much success.

Secondly, there are some highly touted beneficial insects that don't live up to their reputation. The praying mantid is one. Not only is its appetite modest compared with that of other predators, it is nonselective in its feeding habits and will eat almost any insect that passes by, including other beneficials and even its mate.

Only chemical pesticides do an effective job in controlling destructive insects. This little gem of misinformation, fostered by certain chemical companies with a vested interest in promoting the use of their persistent, lethal concoctions, has gotten us into serious trouble with Mother Nature. Undeniably, chemicals generally produce immediate and visible results, but this "kill potential" is proving to be short-lived in a number of cases. Insects are so numerous and durable that often at least a few of any species will be unaffected by even repeated applications of a poison. Those survivors will breed and pass on their resistance to future generations, and soon a new and pesticide-tolerant strain of the insect has evolved. Because most pesticides are nonselective killers, their widespread use can decimate many species of beneficial predators. As a result, we are coping with new generations of chemical-resistant "super bugs" while at the same time having fewer natural predators to keep them in check.

Many organic pesticides, although initially quite deadly, lose their toxicity more quickly than their chemical counterparts, sometimes becoming inert in a matter of hours. This allows beneficials to multiply, so gardeners have both the "good" insects and the organic insecticides working for them against creatures that would damage their crops.

It has taken decades for farmers and orchardists to learn this lesson, but many of them have finally recognized the folly of relying on chemical pesticides and are now turning to organic methods.

CHAPTER 7

Container Farming Tips

❧

IN ESSENCE, CONTAINER GROWING IS NO DIFFERENT FROM horticulture in a traditional garden plot. In both settings, you want to raise healthy food and beautiful flowers. However, a few techniques may vary or take on greater importance with container gardening. Over the years, we have developed a number of productive methods that we find invaluable to insuring success with containers.

Irrigation

Both heat and wind draw moisture from the leaves of fruit and vegetable plants, and unless they are generously watered, the plants will quickly become stressed. This is of particular concern with container-grown plants, whose roots are more exposed to the desiccating elements than plants in garden plots. On scorching, windy days, crops in small containers may need to be watered twice. Otherwise, some of their delicate feeder roots may shrivel and die. Then, instead of concentrating their energy on producing fruit and top growth, the plants must expend themselves to regenerate roots. Container gardeners who want abundant harvests must be regularly attentive to their plants' water needs and keep planting mixes evenly moist during the hot days of summer.

One of the easiest methods of irrigating container crops is to set up a drip system connected to an automatic timer. Water is delivered through what are called emitters, either as a fine spray or a slow drip, directly to the root

One of the easiest methods of irrigating container crops is with a drip system connected to an automatic timer.

zone of your plants, so there is very little waste. You can buy components to design your own drip system or choose from a number of kits. Drip outfits, complete with a timer, several feet of "spaghetti" tubing and a selection of emitter heads, cost between $35 and $50. If you don't need a timer but plan to turn the system on manually, the cost drops to about $20.

The best times to irrigate with a drip system are early morning and early evening, when the sun is less intense. If you use a hose and nozzle sprayer that wets the foliage as well as the soil, irrigate in the morning so the leaves can dry in the warmth of the day. This can reduce the incidence of rot, mildew and other diseases.

Water Conservation

For gardeners living in serious drought areas, there are several techniques you can follow to cut your water use. First, keep a couple of buckets in the bathroom and put one under the tap when you turn on the tub or shower. Collect the water until it warms up enough for you to use. Normally, you can save one to two gallons each day, which will ir-rigate three or four container crops.

Some dedicated water-savers capture the "gray" or rinse water from their washing machines, baths and showers and pipe it into a storage tank. If you use a nonphosphate, low-sudsing detergent, the small residue of soap in the gray water won't harm plants.

Be prepared to collect rainwater, when and if it rains. Have buckets or barrels on hand (you can use inexpensive plastic trash barrels) to set out at the first hint of a sprinkle. Serious water-conservationists hook up the downspout of their gutter system to 50-gallon barrels or other large containers, so they can collect all the precipitation that runs off their roof.

Mulches

Because of the limited soil volume in containers, mixes dry out rapidly. To prevent excessive moisture loss and damage to plants (especially well-established seedlings), cover the soil with a 3- to 4-inch layer of mulch.

There are two broad categories of mulch—organic and inorganic. Organic mulches are biodegradable; they decompose in the soil. They include chipped or shredded bark, compost, lawn clippings, leaf mold and pine needles. Inorganic mulches include plastic, gravel, polyethylene, tin foil and rock chips. Most mulches help keep the mixes cool and moist during hot summer days. An exception is plastic, which has the opposite effect, so it is a good mulch for warm-season crops and for heating up the soil in early spring

Crops that benefit greatly from mulches are those most susceptible to blossom-end rot—eggplants, peppers and tomatoes.

Some of the best mulches for container gardens

are lightweight and inexpensive ones that are commonly available in your area. In the South, these might include cottonseed, peanut and rice hulls; in the East and Midwest, shredded bark, leaf mold and pine needles; in the West, redwood bark and sawdust. Compost, hay and straw are also available in many areas.

You can cut your costs for mulch to almost zero by using newspapers, herbicide- and pesticide-free grass clippings, well-composted yard clippings and vegetable waste from the kitchen.

Heat Stress

With the exception of such tender cool-season crops as lettuce and those that bolt in excessive heat, such as broccoli and cauliflower, all vegetables prosper in full sun—at least six hours of it a day. But there can be too much of a good thing. When the temperature rises above 100 degrees F, nearly all vegetables can become stressed by heat and scorched by the sun. Wilting is a common response to moisture loss. To help your plants through a hot spell, spritz them with the hose and shade them from the intensity of the sun. You can buy shade cloth at most garden centers. It is a durable fabric (usually nylon or plastic) that, depending on the tightness of the weave, filters out from 10 to 90 percent of the sun's light.

Floating row covers can also shade plants somewhat and screen out unwanted insects. However, more heat builds up beneath row covers than under coarsely woven grades of shade cloth. Finally, there is burlap— a natural, biodegradable material that is sometimes more readily available from fabric stores than garden centers. Whatever material you choose, use stakes to create tents over containers so the weight of the fabric doesn't rest on your crops.

Vining Crops

Cucumbers, grapes and brambles do best if trained on a vertical support, such as a trellis. The trellis may need to be secured to a building or fence to keep the plant and container from tipping over. We have found that standard cages don't work well for supporting tomatoes in containers filled with a light mix. The wire frame tends to keel over under the weight of a fruitful plant. Instead, drive four stakes into the mix and wrap twine around the stakes at various heights to support the plant as it grows. For small tomato plants, use one or two stakes and tie the vines loosely to the stakes with plastic garden tape, nylon stockings or strips of cloth.

Vining crops, such as pumpkins and melons, can spill onto the ground around the container. Place a short length of wood or a plastic lid under each fruit to keep it from coming in contact with the soil, which can lead to rot and insect intrusions.

Squashes, gourds and cucumbers do well when trained on plastic netting attached to a fence or other vertical support. Peas and beans, of course, climb merrily up 3- to 6-foot lengths of stout cord. Chicken wire and other metals tend to heat up in the sun and scorch tendrils.

This clever gardener has combined a vegetable growing bag with recycled plastic soda bottles, which are inverted for easy watering access.

Thinning Fruit

Vigorous tomato plants often set fruit in clusters, but sometimes only two or three of these fruits develop well. If you remove the "runts," the remaining tomatoes will be larger and better formed. The same goes for peppers, melons, cucumbers and tree fruits. Thinning helps a plant maximize its energy. It can allow the ripening of a small crop of large, healthy fruit rather than an abundance of small, mediocre ones.

Also, "heading back" or pruning the ends of vines and tomato plants, if they become unruly or if it's getting late in the season, transfers the plant's energy into nurturing the fruit already produced, instead of making more foliage.

Timing

If you pick crops as soon as they are mature, you will encourage plants to continue producing. Leaf lettuce will sprout new leaves, peas will set more pods, tomatoes will concentrate on ripening young fruits. Enjoy broccoli and cauliflower while the heads are firm, leeks and carrots while they are young and tender.

To extend your gardening season, plant fall crops as soon as you harvest warm-season vegetables. Have seedlings of broccoli, cabbage (late), collards, turnips, spinach and radishes ready to drop into containers as soon as you've taken the last of the beans, beets, carrots, corn, cucumbers, peppers and tomatoes. Crops that haven't matured before the onset of cool weather can be kept warm on nippy days with cloches. (See Season Length, this page.)

Companion Planting

Farmers in ancient China may have been among the first to discover that planting certain combinations of herbs and vegetables together created a mutually beneficial environment that encouraged growth and repelled destructive insects. Companion planting is what this approach has come to be called. Several plant combinations may attract beneficials and insect pollinators, as well as enhance the flavor of a crop.

French marigolds produce a strong repellent against nematodes. Garlic or chives in containers of lettuce seem to deter aphids. Radishes combined with cucumbers will sometimes discourage cucumber beetles. Beans planted with collards may reduce aphid infestations on collards.

To attract beneficials and pollinators, plant a few of the following: anise, black-eyed Susans, coreopsis, coriander, caraway, dill, fennel, lovage, santolina, sunflowers and yarrow.

See the chart on the facing page for a few good companion combinations to try.

Another form of companion planting is to interplant fast-growing crops around slow-maturing, erect varieties, thereby maximizing your seasonal harvest. For example, you can grow lettuce or baby carrots around corn, chives or bunching onions around broccoli or Brussels sprouts and radishes around beets, pole beans and onions.

Season Length

The arrival of Labor Day pretty much signals the end of the warm-season vegetables in many parts of the country. In the Northeast, Midwest and mountain states, the last of the tomatoes usually have been harvested by mid-September, and garden tools are being oiled and sharpened in preparation for their winter storage.

But in Florida, along the Gulf Coast, in southern New Mexico and Arizona, and in the coastal and southern California regions, gardening is often a year-round activity. Fall is ideal for growing many of the cool-season crops like cabbage, collards, lettuce, mustard and turnip greens. Cool weather—even a light frost—turns the starch in leaf crops to sugar, producing the sweetest, most tender of these regional gardening favorites.

If you live in the Sunbelt, you can continue to garden and harvest produce right through Christmas and often into spring. Because transplants aren't commonly available after the prime season,

COMPANION PLANTING COMBINATIONS

CROP	COMPANIONS
Asparagus	Basil, Parsley, Tomatoes
Beans	Corn, Cucumbers, Eggplants, Petunias, Potatoes, Radishes, Roses, Sage, Summer Savory
Cabbage Family (Cauliflower, Broccoli, Brussels Sprouts, Collards)	Beans, Celery, Chamomile, Dill, Hyssop, Mint, Nasturtium, Onions, Peppermint, Potatoes, Rosemary, Sage, Thyme
Carrots	Beans, Chives, Dill, Leeks, Lettuce, Marigold, Onions, Radishes, Rosemary, Sage, Tomato, Wormwood
Cucumbers	Beans, Corn, Lettuce, Nasturtium, Peas, Radishes, Sunflower, Tansy, Marigold
Lettuce	Carrots, Cucumbers, Onions, Radishes, Chives, Garlic, Strawberries
Onions	Beets, Broccoli, Chamomile, Carrots, Summer Savory
Peppers (Sweet)	Basil, Okra
Potatoes	Beans, Cabbages, Corn, Eggplant, Horseradish, Marigold
Radishes	Beets, Cucumbers, Lettuce, Marigold, Melon, Nasturtium, Spinach
Squash	Borage, Corn, Nasturtium, Radishes, Tansy
Tomatoes	Bee Balm, Borage, Carrots, Chives, Mint, Nasturtium, Onions, Parsley

you'll have to start your own seedlings in late summer. Since most leaf crops are heavy nitrogen feeders, add 2 parts of well-rotted manure to the standard mix described in Chapter 3 and add a handful of 10-10-10 fertilizer in the lower third of the container to sustain the crops through harvesttime.

Season Extenders

For northern gardeners, the onset of cool fall weather doesn't mean that immature, unharvested crops are lost. You can squeeze another three or four productive weeks from the season by covering your crops with clear plastic. Insert stakes around the inside rim of containers and staple sheets of plastic to these to create an instant greenhouse. Make sure foliage and fruit don't rest against the plastic, or they may rot or be nipped by frost. Leave a gap at the top so excess heat and moisture can escape and air can enter. On warm, sunny days, remove plastic tents and hot caps. At night, if temperatures begin to drop, move containers into the garage or under a carport or overhang.

Small plants can be protected against frost and harsh winds with homemade cloches. Cut the bottom off plastic milk jugs and set them over plants. Remove if the weather warms up.

CHAPTER 8

Spring Spectacular — The Cool-Season Crops

❧

W HILE SUMMER IS THE MOST PRODUCTIVE SEASON in the garden, spring is our favorite time of year because it brings renewal and regeneration after a long winter of inactivity.

Garden centers come alive with shipments of fruit trees and berry plants, pony packs of lettuce, celery and broccoli and seed racks full of the newest varieties and old favorites. Seeds that were started indoors when there was snow on the ground can finally be introduced gradually to the great outdoors. There is a hint of rain in the air, coupled with the aroma of damp earth and the fragrance of early hyacinths.

We begin to compare notes on whom we lent that shovel to last fall and which friend borrowed our favorite trowel and apparently adopted it, finding it, as we did, a lot more comfortable than an old soup spoon. Then, another rite of spring begins—the arrival of catalogs full of seeds and shiny, new gardening toys. And suddenly, our planned canvass of the neighborhood to collect our trusty tools is abandoned.

Temperature has a lot to do with your success in growing container crops. Warm weather and long days stimulate flower and seed production; cool weather and short days promote greater leaf, root and stem growth.

As you might expect, then, root vegetables are cool-season crops. They, and the cool-preference leaf crops, should be planted early enough so they reach maturity before the advent of scorching summer heat or late enough so they are ready for harvest in fall, before the first freeze.

Cole Crops (Cabbage Family)

BROCCOLI. Those who like its distinctive flavor will be happy to know that broccoli is one of the easiest vegetables to grow and that it is a long-term producer.

Types to grow: 'DeRapa', 'Green Comet Fl Hybrid', 'Green Dwarf #36', 'Italian Green Sprouting', 'Raab' and 'Romanesco'.

When/how to plant: Start with young plants from the nursery. In cold-winter areas, you can set out the nursery starts (or your own transplants if you started them from seed) more than two weeks before the last expected frost. Put in a second planting in midsummer for a fall harvest. In mild-winter areas, put in plants from early fall through late winter. You can grow two plants in a 5-gallon container.

Care and feeding: Keep soil evenly moist. Feed with a complete fertilizer at full strength twice during the growing season but before heads begin to form. Broccoli is heat-sensitive and needs consistently cool temperatures. Too much heat forces it to bolt, or flower, and this spoils its eating quality.

Cabbage is a versatile crop and has been called the Spam of the vegetable world.

When to harvest: When heads become deep green and before any yellow florets appear, cut away the head with some stem attached. Once a head is harvested, side shoots will grow out to replace it.

Pests/problems: Aphids, imported cabbage looper, downy mildew and fungus rot. Fungus rot occurs if heads are kept continuously wet or exposed to successive frosts. 'Green Dwarf #36' is tolerant of black rot and mildew.

BRUSSELS SPROUTS. This is another relatively easy vegetable to grow, if you don't live in a part of the country where the summers are long, hot and dry.

Types to grow: 'Burpee Jade Cross E Hybrid', 'Catskill', 'Dolmic Fl Hybrid' and 'Long Island Improved'.

When/how to plant: Since it takes just about four months to mature from seed, you may want to use starter plants. If you pot them in your containers by early June, you'll have sprouts for the table by fall. This one needs plenty of growing room. You'll only get one to thrive in a 3- or 4-gallon container and two in a 5-gallon tub.

Care and feeding: Don't spare the water. Feed when plants are well established and just as sprouts are beginning to form with a complete liquid fertilizer at half strength. As the sprouts begin to cluster, twist off the leaves beneath to transfer growing energy to forming more sprouts.

When to harvest: A well-grown plant will give you about 80 sprouts. Begin harvesting a few at a time before they change color, starting at the bottom of the plant. Frost is not a problem, so your plants should yield good crops for six to seven weeks.

Pests/problems: Aphids, flea beetles and imported cabbage loopers.

CABBAGE. This versatile crop, which has been called the Spam of the vegetable world, can be grown successfully in most of the U.S. It is one of several vegetables that can survive a brief freeze without serious damage.

Types to grow: For early, small heads, try

'Badger Market', 'Copenhagen Market' or 'Emerald Cross'. One of the earliest is 'Early Jersey Wakefield'. For medium-sized heads, try 'Golden Acre', 'Marion Market' and 'Red Ace'. For late crops and large heads, try 'Burpee's Surehead' and 'Danish Ballhead'. An excellent small fall cabbage is 'Minicole Fl Hybrid'.

When/how to plant: Early crops should be timed to reach maturity before the arrival of hot summer days. Fall/winter crops can be started in July. Large-head types require a lot of growing space. Grow one large head in a 2-gallon bucket, three in a 10-gallon container. Lower the soil level a few inches from the rim so young plants are protected from strong winds.

Care and feeding: Cabbage needs abundant and regular water. After transplants have become established, feed every three weeks until heads begin to form with a high-nitrogen, high-potash fertilizer diluted to half strength. Occasionally press additional soil around the stem to encourage new root development. This helps stabilize the plant and hastens maturity.

When to harvest: Take heads when they're uniformly firm to the touch.

Pests/problems: Aphids, cabbageworms, flea beetles and harlequin bugs. Cabbage plants sometimes yellow, and if the weather becomes too hot, their heads may crack. Move containers into shade during hot spells. Heavy feedings of quick-release fertilizer can also cause splitting by spurring a burst of rapid growth.

CAULIFLOWER. If you want a challenge, try growing cauliflower. It's one of the prima donnas of the vegetable kingdom and success with it is uncertain even in the hands of an expert gardener.

Types to grow: 'Early Snowball', 'Snow Crown' (early), 'Snow King' and 'Super Snowball'.

When/how to plant: Plants can require up to three months from seed germination to harvest. Young plants from the nursery mature in about six to eight weeks. If spring in your area is cool, start

To set heads, cauliflower requires frequent deep-watering.

plants in late winter or early spring. In other areas, put seedlings out in early August and grow as a fall crop. Firm soil well around the base of plants. You can grow one plant in a 3-gallon bucket and three in a 5-gallon tub.

Care and feeding: The most common problem encountered when growing cauliflower is its failure to set heads. This can be caused by a sudden heat wave or by dehydration. Cauliflower requires frequent deep-watering and, on dog days, misting to add some humidity. When heads are well formed, tie the outer leaves up over them with twine. This provides protection from the sun and helps the curd to blanch. Feed when plants are well established with a complete fertilizer diluted to half strength and again as curds form.

When to harvest: Examine the cauliflower heads as they begin to mature. They're ready to harvest when the sections begin to separate.

Pests/problems: Aphids, cabbageworms and flea beetles. Heads fail to form as a result of heat or dehydration.

COLLARDS. This traditional southern substitute for cabbage, sometimes called tree cabbage, will do well in nearly every portion of the country. Collards can cope better than cabbage with both heat and cold—in fact, the flavor is enhanced by a light frost. The texture is chewier than cabbage and the flavor is sweeter.

Types to grow: 'Georgia', 'Louisiana Sweet' and 'Vates'.

When/how to plant: Seeds germinate easily and should be sown in early spring and summer about ¼ inch deep. Thin plants so that they are 6 inches apart when leaves are 4 to 5 inches long. Two plants will thrive in a 2-gallon bucket and four in a 5-gallon container.

Care and feeding: Keep plants well watered and

Celery is difficult to grow and requires ample water, a cold spring and a cool early summer.

misted, especially on hot, dry days. Collards require a high-nitrogen, high-potash fertilizer at full strength twice during the growing season.

When to harvest: Most types reach maturity in eight or nine weeks from sowing date, but you can take young leaves earlier, a few at a time.

Pests/problems: Aphids and cabbageworms.

Leaf Crops

CELERY. Like cauliflower, this is one of the most difficult vegetables to grow, even in the hands of an experienced gardener. It benefits from constant attention and cool weather. You may succeed if blessed with a cold spring and cool early summer.

Types to grow: 'Giant Pascal', 'Ventura' and 'Tall Utah 52-70 R Improved'.

When/how to plant: Seeds seemingly take forever to germinate, even after overnight soaking. For the experimental container gardener, we recommend young plants from the garden center. In the few sections of the country that enjoy mild winters, celery can and should be grown for winter harvest. Elsewhere, try late-summer sowing for a fall crop. If you want to try seeds despite their difficulty, barely cover them with mix. Thin when seedlings are 3 to 4 inches tall. One plant will grow in a 2-gallon bucket, five in a 10-gallon container.

Care and feeding: Celery is a bog plant and needs an ample, consistent supply of water. Feed with a complete fertilizer diluted to half strength every two weeks. Mound up soil around the base of each plant (but keep soil out of the center of the stalk) to hasten blanching and stabilize upright growth, which is sometimes a problem with this plant. You can blanch celery quickly by covering it with a paper bag or opaque plastic seven to ten days before harvesting.

When to harvest: You can take tender young stalks a month before maturity. Otherwise, when the plant has blanched, it is ready for harvesting.

Pests/problems: Aphids and celery worms (the larvae of the black swallowtail butterfly). The long growing season (five months from seed, three months from transplants) makes an already difficult plant more of a challenge. Three or four successive nights of temperatures in the 40s can cause the plant to bolt, and this ruins it for the table. Heat, too, is an enemy that can also cause bolting. You can protect celery from cold by using row covers or by moving it indoors until the cold snap breaks. Use shade cloth and misting to protect it against excessive heat. Other problems include western celery mosaic and boron deficiency, which causes browning and cracking of the stalks. 'Tall Utah 52-70 R Improved' is resistant to both of these problems.

CHARD. While celery is difficult, chard is simple and dependable. It hardly needs any special attention and stands up well to rapid temperature changes. Chard thrives virtually anywhere in the continental U.S. and makes a tasty dish, either steamed or in a salad.

Types to grow: 'Fordhook Giant', 'Rhubarb' and 'Ruby'.

When/how to plant: Only in harsh winter areas do you have to worry about sowing schedules. Where winters are severe, sow in May or start seeds four to five weeks earlier indoors. Elsewhere, sow in containers year-round. Seeds should be planted about ½ inch deep. Try one plant in a 2-gallon pot, five in a 10-gallon tub.

Care and feeding: Copious amounts of water during the growing season and a complete liquid fertilizer every two weeks are needed once plants are established. If it gets too little water, the leaves become stiff and coarse. Thin plants when leaves are 2 to 3 inches long and leave 6 inches between remaining seedlings.

When to harvest: Plants mature in two months, but leaves should be taken anytime, as desired.

Pests/problems: Armyworms, flea beetles, leaf miners and some viral diseases.

LETTUCE. Given the high price of lettuce at the market most of the year and the relative ease with which it can be grown, it should be well represented in the container garden. In most areas, well-planned, successive plantings can assure ample

supplies for your salads almost all year long.

Types to grow: LEAF—'Black Seeded Simpson', 'Grand Rapids', 'Red Sails', 'Ruby' and 'Salad Bowl'. CRISP HEAD—'Iceberg'. BUTTERHEAD—

Lettuce can be easily grown and is a good starter crop for children.

'Tom Thumb', 'Baby Bibb' and 'Fordhook'. ROMAINE—'Paris White Cos'.

When/how to plant: Successive plantings from early spring to fall are possible, particularly with starter plants from the nursery. Seeds germinate rapidly. Dribble leaf lettuce seeds in ¼-inch-deep depressions just inside the rim of containers in which you've planted other crops. Thin to every 6 to 8 inches when seedlings emerge. Take leaves as needed. Crisp head, romaine and butterhead plants will eventually need 10 inches between them for optimum growth. Leaf lettuce can be a bit more crowded.

Care and feeding: Plenty of water is needed until heads form, then cut back on frequency and volume. Too much moisture will cause heads to crack. Feed lightly every two weeks with a complete liquid fertilizer diluted to half strength. Lettuce grown into the hot months of summer may wither

Chard thrives virtually anywhere in the continental U.S. and makes a tasty dish, either steamed or in a salad.

or bolt from the heat. Protect plants from the sun with shade cloth.

When to harvest: Leaves can be taken as desired. With most types, when top leaves take on a rusty tinge, maturation is complete.

Pests/problems: Aphids, leafhoppers, tarnished plant bugs, aster yellows, downy mildew, mosaic virus and powdery mildew.

SPINACH. This is a fairly easy crop to grow as long as the weather cooperates. It fails in heat, so a few days with temperatures in the high 80s can cause even a young crop to bolt. But spinach can be a "double cropper," yielding harvests in early summer and late fall if plantings are timed correctly.

Types to grow: 'America', 'Bloomsdale Long-Standing', 'Hybrid No. 7', 'Melody Hybrid' and 'Vienna Hybrid'.

When/how to plant: Start indoors in early spring in peat pots and/or sow outdoors in containers, weather permitting. After the last sweltering days of late summer, a second crop can be started. Seeds should be dropped ½ inch deep and 1 inch apart. You can crowd three plants into a 2-gallon pot and at least ten into a 10-gallon container.

Care and feeding: Keep soil evenly moist throughout the growing season and, once plants are well established, begin feeding with a high-nitrogen fertilizer diluted to half strength every two weeks. When plants are 3 to 4 inches tall, thin so that remaining seedlings are 6 inches apart.

When to harvest: Spinach reaches maturity in four to five weeks.

Pests/problems: Aphids, flea beetles, spinach leaf miners, anthracnose fungus, curly top virus, downy mildew and bolting from heat. New Zealand spinach, or tetragone, is a very heat-tolerant green that can substitute for spinach in the summer garden. 'Melody Hybrid' is resistant to downy mildew and mosaic; 'Vienna Hybrid' is tolerant of downy mildew and spinach blight.

Legumes

PEAS. Peas pose no difficulties, even for the novice. There are few vegetables that taste better than sweet peas eaten within hours of harvesting.

Types to grow: Bush varieties lend themselves well to container gardening, but even tall, or climbing, types can be successfully grown in tubs or pots with twine or trellises for vine support. TALL—'Alderman', 'Melting Sugar', 'Oregon Sugar Pod II' and heat-resistant 'Wando'. BUSH—'Burpee's Blue Bantam', 'Dwarf Gray Sugar' and 'Morse's Progress No. 9'.

When/how to plant: Start seeds indoors or sow

outdoors three weeks before the last expected frost. Fall sowing is recommended for areas with mild winters. Soak container mix and let it drain well, then drop seeds an inch or less deep and 2 inches apart and tamp soil lightly over them. Both climbing and bush types require at least a 10-gallon container for best results.

Care and feeding: Keep soil barely moist. Feed twice during the growing season with a low-nitrogen (5-10-10) liquid fertilizer diluted to half strength. Too much fertilizer stimulates vine and vegetation at the expense of the pods. Thin seedlings to stand 3 inches apart and train climbing types on string, netting or trellises when tendrils appear. (Chicken wire can heat up in the sun and burn tender vines.)

When to harvest: Peas mature in eight to nine weeks after sowing. Harvest pods frequently to encourage plants to set new pods.

Pests/problems: Caterpillars, cucumber beetles, leaf miners, tarnished plant bugs, mites, pea aphids, pea weevils, blight, downy mildew, mosaic virus and powdery mildew. Peas can rot in soil that is consistently cold and wet.

Perennials

ASPARAGUS. The prime reason asparagus is so expensive in the market is that two or three years of patient cultivation are required to produce a crop. If you love this delicious vegetable and are willing to invest the time, you can have your own source for the next 10 years. Harvesting a few spears per plant is possible the second year after they have been planted and several per plant for a decade or so thereafter.

Types to grow: 'Fairbo Hybrid', 'Jersey Giant', 'Martha Washington' and 'Waltham Washington'. For West Coast and southern gardens, try 'UC 157' (two-year-old roots bear first season).

When/how to plant: Instead of growing from seed, save yourself a year's waiting and buy one-year-old plants from the nursery or mail-order house. Avoid any that are wilted or have a poorly developed root structure. (Ask the nurseryman to knock plants out of the container so you can examine the roots.) As soon as the danger of frost has passed, dig a hole 8 inches deep and soak the mix thoroughly. Drop the plant in and firm soil around it. If you're planting roots, plant them so that the tops are 6 inches below the soil line. (You'll need a deep container to do this.) When shoots appear, add more soil but don't cover the growing tips. You can put one or two plants in a 2-gallon pot and up to five in a 10-gallon tub.

Few vegetables taste better than sweet peas eaten within hours of harvesting.

Care and feeding: Water at least every five to seven days during the summer and feed twice a year (early spring and late summer) with a complete liquid fertilizer diluted to half strength. When the leaves begin to brown as winter approaches, cut stems to ground level.

When to harvest: In April or May of the second year, you can begin to cut spears. Cut them when they are 7 to 8 inches tall, using a knife designed for the purpose to avoid injuring plants.

Pests/Problems: Asparagus aphids, asparagus beetles, asparagus miners, snails, slugs, thrips, crown rot, fusarium wilt and rust. 'Jersey Giant' is resistant to crown rot and fusarium wilt.

Root Crops

BEETS. This is one vegetable that can be eaten in its entirety. Although much maligned, beets are a good source of vitamins, almost pest-free and virtually self-tending.

Types to grow: Two especially good choices for containers are 'Little Ball' and 'Red Ace Hybrid'. Others include 'Detroit Dark Red', 'Early Wonder', 'Pacemaker II' (early) and 'Ruby Queen'. For greens, try 'Green Top Bunching'.

When/how to plant: You don't want your crop maturing during the hottest part of the summer, so time your planting to bring a crop in either earlier or later. (Most types mature from seed in two months.) Seeds should be soaked overnight to trigger faster germination. Plant seeds ½ inch deep in moist soil. Seven plants will thrive in a 2- or 3-gallon pot and up to two dozen in a 10-gallon tub.

Care and feeding: Keep soil barely moist throughout the growing season. Thin seedlings when they are 6 inches tall to stand 2 inches apart, then feed with a complete liquid fertilizer diluted to half strength. One feeding is usually sufficient. Keep soil from crusting over by gently cultivating it with a trowel or hand cultivator. Eventually, thin plants so they are spaced 5 inches apart.

When to harvest: Beets mature in eight or nine weeks.

Pests/problems: Aphids, beet armyworms, flea

Insufficient thinning of seedlings will produce beets that are tough, dry and distorted.

beetles, leaf miners, curly top, downy mildew and leaf spot fungus. Slugs and snails will feed on beet tops. Hot weather is an enemy. Oversowing or insufficient thinning produces tough, dry, distorted beets. Beets are subject to nutritional deficiencies (boron, calcium, nitrogen, phosphorus and potassium).

CARROTS. The moist, sweet flavor of freshly picked, home-grown carrots is a world away from the dry taste of most supermarket offerings. Like many other vegetables, commercial carrots are chosen by growers for their ability to stand up to mechanical harvesting—most have strong tops and tough roots, are resistant to diseases and have a long shelf life so they can be refrigerated for months before reaching the marketplace. Because you have none of these concerns, you can grow the "best of the bunch"—carrots that are sweet, tender and loaded with beta carotene, which your body can absorb and convert into vitamin A. Is it any wonder, then, that this easy, rapid producer is a home-grown favorite, despite the relative cheapness of carrots at the market?

Types to grow: There is a variety for every container size. One- to two-gallon buckets are ideal for 'Oxheart' (4 inches), 'French Forcing' (2 inches), 'Gregory Fl Hybrid' (4 inches) and 'Short 'n Sweet' (5 inches); 5-gallon pots are good for 'Half Long' (5 to 6 inches), 'Little Finger' (6 inches), 'Minicor' (5 to 6 inches), 'Nantes' (6 inches), 'Orbit' (round with a 3-inch diameter), 'Red Cored' and 'Royal Chantenay' (both 5 inches); 10-gallon containers provide ample room for a large crop of 'Danvers Half Long' (7½ inches), 'Imperator' (8 inches) and 'Tendersweet' (9 inches). Two late-season varieties to try are 'Autumn King Improved' (10 to 12

You can grow the "best of the bunch"—carrots that are sweet, tender and loaded with beta carotene.

inches) and 'Lange Rote Stumpfe' (8 to 12 inches).

When/how to plant: Carrots do best when started in spring and fall because they prefer the cool of the year. But with ample moisture, they can endure quite a bit of summer heat. Sow directly into containers, about ¼ inch deep. Soil should be moist when seeds are dropped. A thin mulch will prevent the seeds from being washed up during successive irrigations.

Care and feeding: Keep soil barely moist until harvest. Thin seedlings as soon as they can be plucked from the soil and continue thinning until you have 2 inches between the remaining plants. Feed after the final thinning with a complete liquid fertilizer diluted to half strength, and again two to three weeks before harvesting.

When to harvest: Most carrots that are home-grown taste better if eaten a week or more before maturity. Sample as you go.

Pests/problems: Aphids, carrot rust flies, six-spotted leafhoppers, tarnished plant bugs, aster yellows and leaf blights. Successive hot days can wilt seedlings; misting helps keep them moist. Abundant top production and dwarf roots result from inadequate thinning and/or overfeeding.

LEEKS. These members of the onion family are sweet and tasty. They make an excellent base for soups and stews and can be steamed or sautéed as a side dish.

Types to grow: 'King Richard', 'Broad London' ('Large American Flag'), 'Cortina' and 'Titan'.

When/how to plant: Leeks can be sown indoors at least two months before the last frost in your area. To provide a phosphorous-rich growing medium (which leeks prefer), work a pound of bone meal and a cup of slow-release fertilizer, high in phosphorus, into the bottom half of the mix in a 5-gallon container. You can grow about 18 leeks in a 5-gallon tub, 24 in a 10-gallon container.

Care and feeding: Leeks prosper in cool weather. Keep soil evenly moist but never soggy, which can induce rotting. To blanch leeks, mound up soil around them or set a section of 2-inch-diameter plastic pipe over each one when the stems begin to thicken.

When to harvest: Leeks can be eaten anytime, but obviously the longer they are allowed to grow, the larger they will get. With some protection, many varieties will live through even a cold winter and resume growth in the spring. They remain edible for about a month and then become woody, as they begin to go to seed.

Pests/problems: Leeks have many of the same problems and diseases as onions.

ONIONS & GARLIC. Onions can be as inexpensive to buy as to grow. But if you don't grow them, you will never taste the dozens of varieties that are available only from seed. Some of the most flavorful types are not stocked in produce markets because they don't store well. Try other members of the onion family, too, like garlic and shallots.

Dozens of varieties of onions are available only from seed.

Types to grow: 'Italian Red Bottle' and 'Red Tripoli' are seldom-seen varieties. Both are a culinary delight. Also try 'Evergreen Bunching', 'Long White Summer Bunching', 'Yellow Globe Danvers' (firm and strong-flavored), 'Yellow Sweet Spanish' and 'White Sweet Spanish'. One of the sweetest, and a long keeper to boot (6 to 8 months), is 'Sweet Sandwich F1 Hybrid'.

When/how to plant: Plant onion sets (young plants) or seeds in early spring and make successive sowings for continuous supplies. Green onions, garlic and shallots should be planted 1 inch deep and 3 inches apart. You can grow onions in containers of any size, but keep in mind the size of the mature bulb and don't crowd your sets or seeds. Garlic may be started from bulbs purchased at the market. Separate cloves and plant them 3 inches apart in a 5-gallon tub. Fall planting can produce large bulbs by next summer, but in cold-weather regions, protect the crop from freezing by covering containers with an insulating mulch or bringing them into an unheated garage or basement.

Care and feeding: A steady supply of water is essential to good bulb development. Onions are heavy feeders and should be given a 5-10-10 liquid fertilizer at full strength twice a month.

When to harvest: Take green onions as desired. Others have reached maturity when the tops begin to yellow and droop. Spread your harvested onions in the sun for a couple of days and cut off most of the stems before storing.

Pests/problems: Aphids, onion maggots, thrips, downy mildew, fusarium bulb rot, leaf blight, rust and smut. Small bulbs may indicate insufficient watering. 'Long White Summer Bunching' is somewhat resistant to fusarium bulb rot.

RADISHES. These are the easiest of all crops to grow. Raising a box or basket of radishes makes an ideal garden project for children. Radishes are not particular about where they grow, and they mature quickly in three to four weeks from planting. The seeds germinate in about three days. Some radishes grown in the home garden are too hot for most tastes, but you can buy seeds of mild varieties.

Types to grow: SPRING/FALL HARVESTS—'Cherry Belle' (22 days, all red), 'French Breakfast' (24 days, red with white tip) and 'Burpee White' (25 days, white meat). FALL/WINTER HARVESTS—'China Rose' (52 days, hot) and 'White Chinese' (50 days, mild). Radishes tend to bolt in hot weather, but one variety produces well all season (under shade cloth in torrid weather)— 'Crunchy Red Fl Hybrid', a globe type that matures in 22 days.

When/how to plant: Radishes can be planted two to three weeks before the last expected frost or any time other than midsummer in warm-climate areas. Successive sowings should be made every 10 days for as long as radishes are desired. Drop seeds ½ inch deep and 1 inch apart. A dozen will thrive in a gallon pot and you can grow up to three dozen in a 10-gallon tub.

Care and feeding: Ample water on a regular basis produces bumper crops. After plants are established, thin seedlings so that they stand 3 inches apart and feed with a 10-10-10 liquid fertilizer, diluted to half strength. One feeding per crop is all that is needed.

When to harvest: They mature in about a month.

Pests/problems: Cabbage maggots (an occasional problem for the root), cabbageworms and cabbage loopers (which often attack foliage), downy mildew and scab. Failure to thin seedlings may prevent roots from growing to a normal size, producing only a crop of tops.

TURNIPS & RUTABAGAS. These relatives are two of the least popular vegetables, but they are easy to grow and are a good source of vitamins A and C.

Types to grow: TURNIPS—'Just Right Fl Hybrid', 'Purple-Top White Globe', 'Shogoin' (grown for its tops, which are boiled) and 'Tokyo Cross'. RUTABA-

Radishes are not particular about where they grow, and they mature quickly in three to four weeks from planting.

GAS—'American Purple Top' and 'Burpee's Purple-Top Yellow'.

When/how to plant: Turnips mature from seed in about two months, rutabagas in about three months. Sowing should be timed to produce mature crops before or after summer heat. Seeds should be sown just under the soil surface. Soak soil and let it drain before sowing. Both turnips and rutabagas do best in large containers. You should be able to get a good crop of 15 or 16 turnips or rutabagas in a 15- to 20-gallon container.

Care and feeding: Cultural requirements of both turnips and rutabagas are virtually identical. Thin seedlings so that remaining plants are 10 inches apart. Keep soil evenly moist throughout the growing season. Feed only twice—one week after thinning and again three weeks after thinning—with a complete liquid fertilizer, diluted to half strength.

When to harvest: Harvest turnips as soon as they mature. If they are left too long in the soil, they become bitter and fibrous. Take rutabagas when they are 3 to 4 inches thick or leave until fully mature.

Pests/problems: Aphids, cabbage loopers, cabbage maggots, downy mildew and black rot. Small turnips and rutabagas result from oversowing and underthinning.

CHAPTER 9

Summer Bounty— The Warm-Season Crops

❧

WITH THE ARRIVAL OF SUMMER'S SUSTAINED WARMTH, tomatoes that seemed determined to remain eternally green begin to take on color, and melon vines that appeared to be only interested in making more leaves suddenly produce blooms.

Summer is the most productive season in the garden. A combination of heat and long, sunny days results in bumper harvests of tomatoes, squash, melons and corn. There are twice as many warm-season crops as there are cool-season types. Nearly all warm-season crops are aboveground producers because most are sun-lovers.

One of the advantages of farming in buckets is that you can move containers to take maximum advantage of the sun. As the sun rises higher in the summer sky, you can reposition your containers so they are bathed in the sun's rays all day.

Getting Things Off to a Good Start

With the listing for each crop, you'll find specific recommendations for care, from planting to harvest. As a general rule, make sure that seedlings are well watered and out of harsh wind until they are well established. The first few days are crucial to the survival of seedlings, which have only a rudimentary root system. During this crucial period, they are susceptible to dehydration from sultry winds, damage from late frosts and being beaten down by hard rain. Shade cloth or floating row covers draped over stakes driven into containers can protect seedlings from heat and wind until their roots expand into the soil. Both are also good barriers against frost and, if stapled to support stakes, somewhat effective in protecting seedlings from pelting rain.

As you set in seedlings that will eventually need support, such as tomatoes, cucumbers and squash, also install trellises, stakes or netting and twine so you can support vines as they grow. Don't wait to put up supports until the plants are a tangle of growth.

Despite their popularity, tapered tomato cages aren't very efficient for training tomato vines, especially in a light soil mix. We've found they often

Stakes and trellises are needed to support many vegetables and climbing vines.

keel over under the weight of fruit and vine unless stakes are driven in around them to stabilize the cages. The best support for tomato vines is welded wire fencing with 4- to 6-inch grids or the welded wire material used to reinforce concrete. The fencing can be rolled into a cylinder and sunk at least a foot into a container around the plants.

Cheaper and almost as effective are 1-inch-square stakes made of redwood or other rot-resistant wood, driven down to the base of the container. For large, vigorous tomato vines, we set stakes into the container, roughly in a square, and wrap twine around them at varying heights to create a kind of cage. Smaller varieties like 'Patio' can usually be supported by two stakes, one on either side of the plant, with the stems loosely tied to the stakes.

Even peppers and bush-type varieties of beans, cucumbers and peas grow better if securely staked and tied. You can use smaller, thinner stakes than those for tomatoes. Wood and plastic stakes are often sold in bundles at garden centers.

It is crucial to support young vines as they begin to set fruit. Otherwise, they may break. This will reduce not only the size and vigor of the plant but also the size of your harvest. We use lengths of ½-inch-wide plastic tape, available in rolls at most garden centers; it doesn't cut into vines like twine. You can also use old socks, nylon stockings or strips of cloth. Be careful not to tie a vine so tightly that it is strangled or pinched against a stake. Wrap your tie two or three times around the stem, then give the wrapping a little slack when you secure the tie around the stake.

If you are planning to use drip irrigation, you'll want to install the tubing at the beginning of the season. Once crops have developed an abundance of roots and foliage, it is difficult to anchor the tubing and position the emitters where you want them.

If containers are to be placed on a wood deck or other surface that could be stained or damaged by moisture, remember to use horticultural saucers. These should be emptied after you irrigate so containers and plant roots aren't sitting in water.

The following are the most popular and productive of the warm-season crops:

BEANS (LIMA & SNAP). While they are not foolproof, both of these legumes are easy, even for the first-time gardener. Most failures come from sowing seeds too early (seeds will not germinate in cold soil), allowing soil to crust (tender seedlings can't push through caked soil) or allowing the soil to dry out (pods shrivel). Beans are cold-sensitive and should not be planted until after the last expected frost.

Types to grow: Stick with the bush or dwarf varieties for containers. LIMA BEANS—'Burpee Improved Bush Lima', 'Ford Hook No. 242' and 'Geneva'. SNAP BEANS—'Slenderette', 'Bush Blue Lake', 'Derby (R)', 'Greencrop Snap Bush', 'Jumbo', 'Tendercrop', 'Tenderfoot' and 'Tenderette'.

When/how to plant: Sow seeds in late spring and early summer (with the spot or "eye" on the seed coat facing down), 1 inch deep and about 3 inches apart. All types do best in a container of at least 10-gallon capacity. Two plants will flourish in a pot that size.

Care and feeding: Frequent deep-watering is vital to successful crops. After thinning plants to every 6 inches, feed "keepers" with a complete liquid fertilizer diluted to half strength and again when pods begin to form.

When to harvest: To induce plants to produce a second crop and to preserve the flavor and quality of the beans, harvest pods within a week or so after they form. (Check seed packet for maturation time.)

Pests/problems: Aphids, Mexican bean beetles, potato leafhoppers, tarnished plant bugs, bean mosaic, curly top and downy mildew. Shriveled pods result from dehydration. Germination failure is often caused by sowing seeds too early in cold soil. 'Derby (R)' is resistant to bean mosaic virus.

CORN. Although the results aren't always spectacular, corn can be grown in containers on a modest scale. However, pollination can be a problem. In a cornfield, pollination is accomplished by the breeze blowing across row upon row of plants. But there's no rigid rule that corn must be grown in rows. Pollination can occur if at least five plants are grown in a container and two containers are main-

To induce plants to produce a second crop of beans, harvest pods within a week or so after they form.

tained. Ear production may (or may not) be reduced, and the ears themselves may be slightly smaller than normal because of the cramped root space, but the flavor will be just as sweet and the kernels just as tender as field-grown corn.

Types to grow: 'F-M Cross', 'Golden Bantam', 'Kandy Korn', 'Minor Fl Hybrid' and 'Precocious'. For short-season areas and cool coastal climates, try 'Early Extra Sweet', a very sweet variety that matures in about 71 days. 'Honey and Cream' is a tasty bicolor, which produces yellow and white kernels on the same ear. Ask your nurseryman about new dwarf varieties that produce well in confined spaces.

When/how to plant: Sow seeds in late spring (after frost danger) and, in mild-winter areas, again in late summer for a fall crop. Drop seeds 1 inch deep in well-watered and well-drained soil. We grow four standard-sized varieties in a 15-gallon container and six in a 30-gallon tub. Six bantam types can be grown in a 15-gallon pot.

Care and feeding: At least eight hours of sun each day are needed to produce the best crops, but adequate harvests can be had under less ideal conditions if you select hybrids suited to your area. Thin plants to one every foot, then water thoroughly. Continue watering about twice a week, especially if weather has been hot and dry. Water containers deeply when tassels and silk appear. Feed with a 5-10-10 fertilizer at full strength every three weeks.

When to harvest: When the silk turns dark and dries, the ears are ready to check for maturity. Peel back the husk and press a kernel with your thumbnail. If it squirts a milky fluid, it's ready. (Twist, don't pull, ears from the stalk.)

Utilizing vertical space increases the harvest and adds visual interest to container plantings.

Pests/problems: Aphids, corn earworms, corn rootworms, flea beetles, seed-corn beetles, seed-corn maggots, southwestern corn borers, corn smut, maize dwarf mosaic, northern/southern corn blight and rust. Chances are, you will be able to avoid most of the pests and problems farmers encounter because of the small size of your crop. Aphids and corn earworms may, however, home in on your corn plants.

CUCUMBERS. This sun-lover is one of the easiest of the vine crops to grow, but it is susceptible to a number of diseases and pest invasions. There are disease-resistant hybrids you can grow to enhance your chances for a productive crop.

Types to grow: 'Burpee Hybrid II', 'Burpee Pickler' (pickling), 'H-19 Little Leaf', 'Bush Champion' (compact, all-weather producer), 'Marketmore', 'Salad Bush Hybrid' (compact, ideal for containers) and 'Victory'.

When/how to plant: When temperatures rise to a constant 60 degrees F, make your first planting. Follow in a month with a second planting to provide for ample harvests throughout the summer. You can grow one compact type in a 5-gallon container and a standard variety in a 7- to 10-gallon size. If banana-shaped cucumbers are a problem, train your plants on a trellis or netting. Cucumbers that hang from the vine tend to grow straight.

Care and feeding: Cucumbers like an evenly moist growing medium and warm soil. You can mulch with black plastic until the weather heats up, then switch to aluminum foil; this not only reflects heat but reflects light under the foliage, which discourages aphids. Feed with a high-phosphorus fertilizer diluted to half strength when plants begin to flower and every other week thereafter.

When to harvest: Take cucumbers while they're young. Frequent harvesting spurs greater fruit production. First harvests can usually be made five to six weeks after planting.

Pests/problems: Aphids, cucumber beetles, squash bugs, squash vine borers, alternaria blight, bacterial wilt, black rot, downy mildew, mosaic and powdery mildew. 'Burpee Hybrid II' is resistant to downy mildew, mosaic; 'Salad Bush Hybrid' is tol-

Along with improved yields, many new hybrids bring vibrant color and endearing shape to the garden. Left to right: 'Purple Husk' corn, 'Bambino' eggplant, 'Hybrid Burpless' cucumber.

erant of downy mildew, leaf spot, mosaic, powdery mildew and scab.

EGGPLANT. This is not only a versatile vegetable, but it is also an attractive plant when it is heavy with colorful fruit. It is not an easy plant to grow but it's not that difficult either if you live in an area where summers are long and hot.

Types to grow: Good container types are 'Black Magic Hybrid', 'Early Beauty Hybrid', 'Jersey King', 'Morden Midget', 'Oriental Egg' (white, egg-shaped) and 'Slim Jim'. Two varieties that are tolerant of tobacco mosaic virus are 'Dusky Hybrid' and 'Vernal'. (Consult your nurseryman for the best types to try in your locality.)

When/how to plant: Because they require a long season, start with young plants from the nursery. If these are unavailable, start seeds in peat pots indoors (two seeds to a pot, dropped ½ inch deep) at least a month (two months in northern areas) before you plan to transfer them to outdoor containers. Seeds germinate best when the soil temperature is in the mid-80s. Transplant about two weeks after the date of the last expected frost. You can grow three or four plants in a 10-gallon container.

Care and feeding: Sun, sun and more sun. Once plants are established, water heavily once a week and feed monthly with a complete fertilizer diluted to half strength. If soil dries out rapidly, increase frequency of irrigation. Soil must be evenly moist throughout the growing season. Protect plants on cool nights by covering them with plastic or row-cover material or by moving containers into a warm environment. Cool weather stunts growth and reduces yield.

When to harvest: Most types are tastier if harvested young—two or three weeks before maturity. Press eggplant with your thumb. If the dent remains, it's time to pick. Early harvesting usually induces the plant to produce a bigger crop later on.

Pests/problems: Aphids, Colorado potato beetles, flea beetles, hornworms, whiteflies, anthracnose, fusarium and verticillium wilts and tobacco mosaic virus. If the plant becomes top-heavy with fruit, stake and tie as you do tomatoes.

HORSERADISH. This is a fairly deep-rooted Old World perennial but, nonetheless, it can be easily grown in a 5-gallon or larger container. Freshly made horseradish is considerably tastier and more pungent than most commercially processed products.

Types to grow: The most popular cultivated variety is 'Maliner Kren'.

When/how to plant: Horseradish rarely produces viable seed. The standard method of starting the plant is by vegetative propagation (taking root cuttings from established plants). These are available from mail-order nurseries and garden centers in early spring. After the danger of frost has passed, bury cuttings 2 inches deep, at a slight angle, in a humus-rich mix. Grow one plant per 5-gallon container.

Care and feeding: Keep soil mix evenly moist. Feed once during the season with a complete fertilizer at full strength.

When to harvest: Portions of the roots may be taken during the summer, as desired. The traditional practice is to lift the roots in fall after the first frost. But plants may be overwintered, if the soil in the container is kept from freezing. They will regenerate in the spring. In fact, in some gardens, horseradish can become invasive but this is not a concern in container growing.

Pests/problems: Horseradish is generally a problem-free crop.

JÍCAMA. Also called yam bean, this frost-tender perennial from the Amazon Basin produces large, edible tubers that require about six months of warm, frost-free weather to mature. Although jícama can be steamed or boiled, it is most often peeled, diced and used in salads for its crunchy texture and mild flavor, which are reminiscent of water chestnuts.

Types to grow: Jícama is not sold under varietal names. Seeds are available from a few mail-order firms, including Mellinger's.

When/how to plant: Because of its need for several months of warm weather, the best regions for growing tubers of ample size are the frost-free sections of the southern U.S. In the rest of the country and Canada, start seeds indoors as much as three months before plants can be safely set out in containers. Jícama's vining foliage, which is poisonous, can be trained on a trellis or allowed to spill over the

Jícama produces large, edible tubers that require about six months of warm, frost-free weather to mature.

sides of the container. One jícama can be grown in a 3- to 5-gallon tub.

Care and feeding: Jícama requires at least six hours of direct sun each day and soil that is evenly moist but not soggy. Feed with a 10-10-10 liquid fertilizer at full strength once during the growing season.

When to harvest: Small tubers, which are tastier and more tender than fully mature ones, may be taken at the end of the summer in regions where fall frost would kill the foliage. In frost-free zones, harvest in October or November. Where fall or winter weather is harsh, plants may be carried along a few months indoors in a warm greenhouse.

Pests/problems: Jícama has a built-in pesticide in

its flowers and foliage. Both are toxic to insects, animals and people.

MELONS. With the recent introduction of early-maturing varieties of melons, even northern gardeners can grow these luscious and healthful taste treats. As long as they are planted in an open, sunny location, they're largely trouble-free. Many new dwarf vine or bush cultivars have been developed, which makes growing melons in a container very easy.

Types to grow: CANTALOUPES—especially in the north, try 'Sweetheart Fl Hybrid' (65 days, a pink-fleshed, sweet-flavored oval fruit) and 'Sweet 'n Early Hybrid' (75 days, with juicy salmon flesh, very sweet flavor and round to oval fruit). Varieties perfect for large containers are 'Bush Star Hybrid' (with oval 4- to 5-inch fruit), 'Honeybush' (which produces three to six melons weighing 2½ to 3 pounds) and 'Minnesota Midget' (an early-maturing melon that produces many sweet-flavored 4-inch melons). Four other prolific producers are the aromatic 'Ambrosia Hybrid', 'Burpee Hybrid' (which produces 4- to 5-pound melons), the compact 'Musketeer' (with several 5½- to 6-inch round fruits) and the compact Israel-bred 'Ogen' (which has sweet, aromatic green flesh). Another Israeli introduction, whose seeds are available only by mail from Nichols Garden Nursery, is 'Gallicum' (which has sweet flesh that is light green when ripe).

HONEYDEWS—these juicy melons generally have lime-green flesh, but 'Amber Hybrid' has orange flesh with a nectar-sweet flavor. Each vine produces four to six melons that average 9 pounds. Two good candidates for northern gardeners are 'A-One Hybrid' (80 days, with a sweet, pear-like flavor) and 'Venus Hybrid' (88 days).

WATERMELON—northerners should try 'Fordhook Hybrid' (74 days, with melons that average 12 pounds, and 'Golden Crown F1 Hybrid' (60 days, with oval melons weighing 6 to 8 pounds that have sweet, crimson flesh and yellow skin at maturity). Ideal for containers are 'Bush Baby II Hybrid' (dwarf plants with round 10-pound fruits), 'Bush Sugar Baby' (with 3- to 4-foot vines and melons averaging 10 pounds), 'Golden Midget' (an early type with skin that turns greenish yellow when ripe and that produces several melons weighing about 6 pounds) and 'Yellow Baby Hybrid' (a sweet, yellow-fleshed variety with melons up to 10 pounds). There are dozens of watermelon varieties from which to choose.

When/how to plant: Northern gardeners should start seeds indoors in peat pots 4 to 6 weeks before setting them out in containers. Plants will need to be hardened-off, or gradually introduced to cool weather. In the Sunbelt, where the growing season is long, gardeners can plant seeds outdoors after weather warms to about 60 degrees F. Nevertheless, starting seeds in peat pots is recommended so that transplants are growing vigorously when you set them out into containers. Grow one plant in a 5-gallon pot and two in a 10- to 15-gallon container.

If melons smell aromatic and sweet, they are ready to harvest.

Care and feeding: All melons thrive in warm temperatures. In relatively cool, short-season areas, keep soil mix warm by covering it with black plastic and position containers where they can get direct sun all day. We let our vines spill out onto the ground and take care not to step on the forming melons. However, vines grown in large, heavy containers can be trained on a trellis or sturdy stakes. Trellises will likely cause small containers (5-gallons or less) to tip over, unless they are staked in the ground or secured to a fence or other structure.

Depending on their size, melons can sometimes be supported with netting, cheesecloth or nylon stockings tied to a trellis. Keep mix moist, but be aware that overwatering can cause fruit to crack and may reduce sugar content. Keep foliage dry to avoid disease problems.

Scratch a small handful of slow-release 10-10-10 fertilizer into the soil after vines flower and side-dress with a water-soluble fertilizer a couple of weeks before the first harvest.

When to harvest: There are two time-honored tests for determining melon maturity. First, press a thumb against the blossom end. If there is give, the melon is probably ripe. To be certain, sniff the melon. If it smells aromatic and sweet, it's ready. Some melons change color and others slip easily off the vine when mature.

Pests/problems: Aphids, cucumber beetles, mites, squash bugs, vine borers, anthracnose, bacterial wilt, black rot, blight, downy mildew, fusarium wilt, mosaic disease and powdery mildew. 'Sweet 'n Early Hybrid' and 'Amber Hybrid' are resistant to powdery mildew; 'A-One Hybrid' is resistant to fusarium wilt and powdery mildew.

OKRA. This southern favorite is ornamental as well as edible, particularly the All-America Selections winner,

'Burgundy', which has red stems and fruit, red-veined leaves and yellow flowers.

Types to grow: Besides 'Burgundy', try 'Blondy' and 'Lee', which are both compact 3-foot-tall plants, and 'Clemson Spineless', another All-America Selections winner.

When/how to plant: Wait for nights to warm to an average of 65 degrees F before sowing seeds. Germination is better if seeds are soaked overnight in warm water. Add bone meal at the rate of 2 tablespoons per gallon of mix before sowing to provide extra phosphorus.

Okra loves warmth. After seedlings emerge, mulch topsoil with black plastic.

Care and feeding: Full sun and evenly moist soil produce the best crops. During cold snaps, cover

Peppers are prolific and make handsome porch plants.

plants with floating row cover or clear plastic. Grow one plant in a 5-gallon or larger container.

When to harvest: Most varieties mature in less than two months. Harvest regularly. Younger pods are more tender.

Pests/problems: Aphids, caterpillars, corn earworms, stink bugs and southern blight.

PEPPERS. Here's one vegetable you can treat as a houseplant—if you have a sunny location for it. Most bell, sweet, chili and dwarf varieties thrive indoors or out.

Types to grow: BELL—'Bell Boy', 'Cadice', 'Purple Beauty', 'Select California Wonder', 'Sweet Chocolate', 'Titan' and 'Yolo Wonder'.

CHILI—'Long Red Chili', 'Fresno Chili', 'Long Red Cayenne', 'Mexibell Hybrid' and 'Red Chili; blistering-hot varieties include 'Habanero', 'Scotch Bonnet', 'Serrano' and 'Tabasco'.

SWEET—for a nice display of sweet peppers in a variety of shapes, colors and sizes, try the blush-skinned 'Aconcagua', the red or yellow 'Corno di Toro', 'Italian Sweet', 'Jimmy Nardello' and 'Paprika', as well as standard favorites like 'Early Prolific', 'Sweet Banana' and 'Sweet Cherry' (pickling); in short-season regions, grow 'Cubanelle' and 'Italian Sweet'.

DWARF—'Jingle Bells', 'Little Dipper Hybrid' (thumb-sized sweet red peppers ideal for salads).

When/how to plant: Pepper seeds are difficult to germinate. The most effective method is to sow them in seed flats or peat pots and cover with plastic wrap at least eight weeks before you plan to set them out. Some gardeners use heating coils to warm the soil in seed flats and encourage germination. Seeds should be sown ½ inch deep. Transplants from the nursery are easier but selection is limited.

Peppers, like okra, are warmth-lovers, so wait for the cool spring weather to pass before setting out plants. Space plants 10 to 12 inches apart. Large bell types need at least 3 gallons of container space per plant. Some smaller chili plants will grow in less space.

Care and feeding: Water every week and feed with a complete fertilizer diluted to half strength when plants are well established and once more just before blossoms open. Ideal temperatures for peppers are 68-degree-F nights and 75- to 80-degree-F days. Use a floating row cover or shade cloth to protect fruit from sunscald if the weather turns torrid (over 90 degrees F).

When to harvest: Take peppers as soon as they reach usable size to encourage greater fruit production. Full maturity, when peppers reach a deep red or yellow color, can take 12 weeks from transplanting. Cut, don't pull, peppers when picking to avoid injuring the plant.

Pests/problems: Aphids, corn earworms, European corn borers, flea beetles, hornworms, pepper maggots, pepper weevils, whiteflies, bacterial spot, fusarium and verticillium wilts and tobacco mosaic virus. Erratic watering can cause blossom-end rot. Harsh winds and high temperatures can cause blossom drop. Low temperatures can prevent fruit from setting. 'Select California Wonder' is resistant to tobacco mosaic virus.

POTATOES. "Spuds" have become a popular home-garden vegetable in the last few years. They're a cinch to grow and, with all the novelty types available, they're also fun—particularly for kids. Most garden varieties used to be plain old white. Now, you can have blue-skinned types with lavender flesh, red-skinned with pink flesh and brown with yellow flesh. There is even one with blue meat. One mail-order source in Idaho (where else?) offers more than 100 varieties.

Types to grow: 'Charlotte', 'Kennebec' (a popular, all-purpose variety), 'Red Pontiac' (an all-purpose variety that is a long-keeper) and 'Irish Cobbler' (early and versatile). Among the novelty types, try 'All Blue' (lavender flesh), 'Bintje' (yellow flesh), 'Blossom' (pink meat) and 'Ruby Crescent' (a fingerling with yellow flesh).

When/how to plant: Order certified disease-free seed potatoes in late winter and start them in containers at the first hint of spring. Potatoes are cold-tolerant, so you shouldn't worry about light frosts early in the season. Some seed potatoes are planted whole; larger ones should be cut into sections. (Make sure each section has at least one eye.) Give

Seed potatoes should contain at least one "eye." Give cut pieces a day or two to callus, then plant them about 4 inches deep, 7 inches apart. Hilling plants as they grow encourages tuber production along the buried stem.

the cuts a day or two to callus over before planting. Use a 15- to 20-gallon container or half whiskey barrel and sprinkle a handful of slow-release 10-10-10 fertilizer in the soil in the bottom third of the container. Fill the tub only half full, then drop in potatoes, eyes up, spacing them about 7 inches apart. Cover with 4 inches of soil mix. As the foliage appears, mound up more mix, covering the stems but not the foliage. Potatoes will form along the stems in these mounds. After a few weeks, the container will be filled and you can allow the tops to rise and go to flower.

Some gardeners remove the blossoms, reporting that this induces the plant to produce better harvests; other growers have found no increase in yield.

In another popular technique, the potatoes are planted as previously described, then straw is mounded over the plants. This makes harvesting a little easier and requires less soil mix.

Care and feeding: A sunny location is imperative. Keep the soil mix evenly moist. Drought-and-drench cycles create deformed tubers.

When to harvest: Take small potatoes any time. For a complete harvest, wait until tops die.

Pests/problems: Aphids, blister beetles, Colorado potato beetles, flea beetles, leafhoppers, bacterial ring rot, early/late blight and scab. 'Kennebec' is resistant to blight.

PUMPKINS. This decorative and tasty member of the squash family is one of the most versatile vegetables you can grow. Its flesh, although sometimes stringy, is used for cooking, its seeds provide a healthful snack and its shell is, of course, used to carve out festive Halloween jack-o'-lanterns. You can grow one vine in a 5-gallon tub, allowing the vine to cascade onto the ground. Place a board under each pumpkin to avoid rot and insect damage.

Types to grow: 'Autumn Gold Hybrid' (each vine yields three to five pumpkins of 8 to 10 pounds each), 'Bushkin' (a compact 5- to 6-foot vine with one to three fruits each weighing 8 to 10 pounds), 'Jack Be Little' (eight to ten baby pumpkins on a compact vine), 'Jack-O'-Lantern' (the best for carving, with fruit 8 to 10 inches across), 'Small Sugar' (commonly called "New England Pie Pumpkin" for it has sweet, meaty flesh), 'Spirit Hybrid' (another with compact vines and medium-sized fruit) and 'Triple Treat' (also a good candidate for carving, producing 6- to 8-pound fruits).

When/how to plant: Sow seeds in containers after the danger of frost has passed. Grow only one vine in a 5-gallon or larger container.

Care and feeding: Cover plants with row cover until flowers appear, then remove when bees are active for pollination. Give pumpkins deep irrigation (don't wet leaves) when soil dries out to a depth of 3 inches (may be daily in hot weather) and feed after blooming with a 10-10-10 fertilizer at full strength.

When to harvest: Most pumpkins turn a deep orange when mature, although one or two varieties are white-skinned. Snip off fruit with pruning shears, taking 3 or 4 inches of stem along with the pumpkin.

Pests/problems: Aphids, cucumber beetles, mites, squash bugs, squash vine borers, angular leaf spot, bacterial wilt, downy mildew, mosaic, powdery mildew and scab.

SQUASH. All squashes grow well in containers. Vining types can be trained on trellises or allowed to spill out of containers.

Types to grow: SUMMER—'Burpee's Fordhook Zucchini', 'Clairimore Lebanese' (zucchini), 'Gold Rush' (zucchini), 'Green Magic' (zucchini), 'Pasta Hybrid' (cylindrical spaghetti), 'Pic-N-Pic Hybrid' (crookneck), 'Poly-Poly' (round zucchini, can be eaten raw), 'Sunburst Hybrid' (scallop) and 'Sun Dropps Hybrid' (oval).

WINTER—'Burpee's Butterbush' (bush butternut), 'Bush Acorn Table King' (acorn), 'Buttercup', 'Cream of the Crop Hybrid' (acorn) and 'Orangetti Fl Hybrid' (semibush spaghetti).

When/how to plant: Start seeds indoors for planting after the danger of frost has passed. In the North, use black plastic mulch to warm the soil. Keep seedlings covered with a floating row cover until plants blossom. Mulch with aluminum foil to deter squash vine borers, a prime enemy. Plant two vining types in a 10-gallon or larger container. In southern areas, winter squash should be started in late summer either from transplants or by directly sowing in the container.

Care and feeding: Keep the mix evenly moist and try to keep water off the foliage, which is susceptible to mildew. Use organic mulch covered with aluminum foil to conserve moisture. Feed with a 10-10-10 fertilizer after fruit sets. A sunny location is vital to good fruit production.

When to harvest: Take summer squashes when young and tender. Harvest winter types when fully mature, removing some of the stem with the fruit.

Pests/problems: Aphids, cucumber beetles, mites, squash bugs, squash vine borers, alternaria blight, bacterial wilt, downy mildew, leaf spot, mosaic and powdery mildew.

SWEET POTATOES. Although only served at holiday time in some parts of the country, sweet potatoes are a popular year-round dish in the South. They are a trouble-free crop and one of the easiest to grow, but they do require a long season to mature.

Types to grow: The best variety for container culture is 'Porto Rico', a vineless bush type. It has coppery orange skin and flesh that is slightly red; average maturity is 120 days. One of the most popular varieties is 'Centennial', which, although developed for southern gardens, prospers in the North

Sweet potatoes are a trouble-free crop but require a long growing season.

and Midwest. Roots (potatoes) are orange-skinned and the moist, sweet flesh is deep orange. Other varieties to try are 'Allgold' (cans and stores well), 'Jewel' (good storer), 'Nancy Hall' (sometimes called white yam) and 'Vardaman' (productive bush type).

When/how to plant: There are three sources for transplants—garden centers (in the South), mail-order nurseries and your own seed flats. To grow your own transplants, called "slips" or "draws," pick out a few sweet potatoes at your local market in early spring. Chose medium-sized, firm roots with no deep gouges or blemishes. You can either suspend the potato in a glass of water with toothpicks stuck in the sides or bury the root lengthwise to half its depth in a pot of soil mix, sand and compost that you keep just barely moist. Set the containers in a bright, warm spot near (but not in) a sunny window. Sprouts with tiny rootlets will form from dormant eyes. Once these are about 8 inches tall, snip them off, leaving a stem 1 inch long attached to the potato.

Use a 20-gallon tub or half whiskey barrel to grow sweet potatoes. Fill the container with humus-rich planting mix to about 10 inches below the rim and build a mound in the center. Insert slips an inch deep into the mound, spaced about a foot apart. Keep the transplants well watered and shaded until they are growing vigorously.

Care and feeding: After transplants are established, keep the mix just barely moist. A month after setting in slips, sprinkle a 10-10-10 slow-release fertilizer around the plants but not in contact with the stems.

When to harvest: Most varieties require about four months to reach their mature size, but you can harvest younger potatoes after 100 days. In areas where frost is common, harvest all potatoes before vines are frost-killed. Dig carefully to avoid bruising the roots. Select blemish-free keepers for storage and as seed potatoes for next season.

Pests/problems: Container growing eliminates one of the biggest threats to sweet potatoes—nematode damage. In the South, sweet potato weevils are also a problem. When buying slips, insist on certified weevil-free transplants. To control infestation, keep containers free of debris and don't use the planting mix again.

TOMATILLA (Husk Tomato). Tomatillas are staples in Latin-American countries, where they are crushed and blended in sauces. The plants resemble those of tomatoes, except that the slightly tacky fruits (about 2 inches in diameter) are encased in papery husks that split open when the fruit is mature.

Types to grow: Because tomatillas are relatively new in commerce, they are not available by varietal name, but the seeds are carried by many seedsmen.

When/how to plant: Sow seeds indoors a month before the last frost date. Mix 2 tablespoons of superphosphate in the bottom layer of soil in a 5-gallon container. Grow one plant per container.

Care and feeding: A full day of direct sun and barely moist soil produce the best plants.

When to harvest: Once husks split, fruit is mature (late August to early September). Fruit is ready if it has a slight give to it when pressed between thumb and forefinger. You can ripen hard fruits by setting them on a windowsill.

Pests/problems: Tomatillas are largely pest- and disease-free.

TOMATOES. Without a doubt, tomatoes are the most popular garden vegetable. They are easy, productive and inexpensive (unlike their market counterparts), and they adapt well to container cultivation. There are scores of prolific varieties, ranging from the tiny cherry to the huge beefsteak types, and dozens of novelty cultivars, from the yellow pear to the striped, acid-free white ones.

Types to grow: In areas where summers are cool, try one of the following four types: EARLY—'Burpee's Early Pick Hybrid VF', 'Good 'n Early Hybrid VFT' and 'Fireball'. MIDSUMMER—'Heinz 1350', 'Gardener's Delight' (cherry), 'Jim Dandy Hybrid', 'Red Cherry' (cherry), 'Super Marmande', 'Supersweet 100' (cherry), 'Tigerella' (striped) and 'White Wonder' (a low-acid white tomato). LATE SUMMER—'Ace 55', 'Early Pak 7', 'Pearson Improved' and 'Super Roma'. TOMATOES ESPECIALLY FOR CONTAINERS—'Basket King Hybrid', 'Golden Pygmy', 'Patio Prize VFN', 'Red Robin', 'Tiny Tim' and 'Tom Thumb'.

When/how to plant: If you want to start from seed, sow them ½ inch deep indoors about two months before the last hard frost is due. Starter plants from the nursery are the most convenient, but variety selection is very limited. Transplant to

Pick tomatoes just before they mature and let them reach peak ripeness on a windowsill.

containers outdoors about two weeks after the last expected frost. Plants should be buried so that their lowest leaves are just above the soil surface. Roots will develop from the buried portion of the stem and give the plants additional stability. Tomatoes are heavy feeders. Mix 2 tablespoons of pelletized limestone per gallon of soil to provide extra calcium and help prevent blossom-end rot. Give them plenty of room for their roaming roots, which grow to 6 feet and longer. A 10-gallon tub is good for one large variety, but a 15- to 20-gallon container is even better.

Care and feeding: If temperatures remain around 90 degrees F, deep-watering every other day may be needed. The soil should be kept barely moist. Feed with a low-nitrogen, high-phosphorus food (or a specially formulated tomato food) once a month while tomatoes are developing. Once you begin harvesting, stop feeding. Additional fertilizer will only stimulate healthy foliage at the expense of fruit production. Cultivated tomatoes are almost universally self-pollinating. But if plants are sheltered from the wind, you may need to rock the container or tap the stakes to ensure that pollen drops from the anthers onto the stigma in each flower.

When to harvest: Let tomatoes almost ripen on the plant, then remove them with a bit of the stem attached and let ripening continue on a windowsill. Fully ripened tomatoes lure insects, rodents, raccoons and other nocturnal critters.

Pests/problems: Aphids, Colorado potato beetles, flea beetles, hornworms, mites, anthracnose, bacterial canker, fusarium and verticillium wilts, late blight, southern bacterial wilt and tobacco mosaic virus. Failure to set fruit may be caused by many problems, primarily too much nitrogen in the soil, excessive shade, rain and humidity and successive cool days and nights. Most of these are in the hands of Mother Nature. However, blossom-end rot, indicated by tough black spots on the bottom of the fruit, can be minimized by putting lime in the soil mix to boost the availability of calcium and by keeping the mix evenly moist. A mulch of straw, plastic or ground bark will help keep moisture from evaporating between waterings.

Cracking is another moisture-loss problem that can also be corrected by mulching. Yellowing foliage usually means an iron or nitrogen deficiency, a common problem with plants that need copious amounts of water. There are iron and nitrogen additives on the market to correct the problem.

Tomatoes need healthy foliage to carry out photosynthesis. 'Burpee's Early Pick Hybrid VF' is resistant to fusarium and verticillium wilts; 'Good 'n Early Hybrid VFT' is resistant to fusarium and verticillium wilts and tobacco mosaic virus.

CHAPTER 10

Beautiful Berries, Fabulous Fruit

❧

IMAGINE THE PLEASURE YOU'LL GET FROM PICKING YOUR OWN berries and fruit at their peak of ripeness. No longer will you have to settle for frozen fruits that have been robbed of their flavor by long refrigeration. By growing your own, you will have an ongoing supply of fresh offerings for the fruit salad—for a fraction of their supermarket cost. You can grow frost-tender tropicals, too, like figs and citrus, even if you live in the Northeast.

Don't be intimidated by what you may have heard about the difficulty of growing fruit trees. We find them less demanding than many vegetables that need frequent feeding, watering, trellising and pest control. Some—like apples—do require a pollinator, so you'll need to plant a second variety that blooms at the same time. But most are self-fruitful and will bear a bountiful crop without cross-pollination.

Some fruit trees need to be sprayed in the late winter with what is called dormant oil. This is a simple procedure, but it may be unfamiliar to some gardeners. You don't need elaborate equipment. You can use a hand mister or buy a small garden sprayer, which sells for less than $15. While the tree is dormant, you apply an even coat of oil to the tree's branches and trunk. This will effectively smother the damaging insects that overwinter in the bark.

We grow seven different kinds of fruit trees and feel that the harvests we enjoy are well worth the effort. We think that if you put in a few fruit trees, you'll soon agree.

Berries

Growing berries in containers is slightly more work than growing them in the garden. Trellising and selective pruning may be necessary to keep canes of bramble types from taking over the space you've allocated, but these chores are sometimes required even when berries are established in the yard.

Berries are generally sold as bare-root plants. They are not in a container and have no dirt around their roots. Their roots are packed in moist sawdust, peat moss or a combination of the two and then wrapped in plastic packaging. Some nurseries set their plants in bins of compost, peat or sawdust, so you can see the condition of the roots before you buy. Once in a while, berries are also sold in containers or as balled-and-burlapped (B&B) specimens. These are often more expensive than bare-root plants.

Bare-root or B&B plants, such as blueberries, currants and gooseberries, that don't sell right away are usually planted in containers and set out again for the next gardening season. Brambles are generally discounted until they find a buyer. They are not normally potted and sold later because they have such an unruly growth habit. These "distressed" plants can be a bargain, if they were properly cared for and their roots were kept moist.

BLUEBERRIES (HIGHBUSH & RABBITEYE). Blueberries have an undeserved reputation for being difficult to grow. The fact is, if their modest needs are met, they're no more trouble than tomatoes. In addition to delectable berries, you'll get a decorative ornamental with pinkish white flowers and foliage that turns a bright crimson in the fall. If you live in the Northeast, where blueberries do best, you should grow the hardy, cool-preference highbush type. Southern and Sunbelt gardeners are generally limited to the heat-tolerant rabbiteye varieties.

Types to grow: HIGHBUSH (zones 4 to 8)—'Bluecrop' (midseason), 'Blueray' (early midseason), 'Earliblue' (early), 'Herbert' (late), 'Jersey' (late), 'Northland' (early midseason). RABBITEYE (zones 7 to 9)—'Centurion' (late), 'Delite' (midseason), 'O'Neal' (early, needs no pollinator), 'Premier' (early), 'Tifblue' (midseason) and 'Woodard' (early).

When/how to plant: Because blueberries need a pollinator to produce abundantly, you'll have to plant two different varieties that bloom at the same time—for example, two early-season cultivars or two late-season types. Bare-root blueberries should be planted in early spring or late fall. You can plant B&B or container-grown bushes any time from spring through fall. (See Dwarf Fruit Trees, page 104, for planting techniques.) You should use a container with at least a 10-gallon capacity.

Care and feeding: A full day of sun produces the biggest harvests, but blueberries will set fruit in a half day of direct sun. Use the acidic soil mix recommended for berries on page 26. Keep the mix evenly moist. Blueberries need a constant supply of water, especially after berries are set. They are fairly shallow-rooted and benefit from the cooling effects of a blanket of organic mulch of oak leaf mold, pine needles or peat. Don't fertilize blueberries in their first season. The following year, feed a 10-10-10 fertilizer before flower buds open and monthly until you harvest the last of the berries.

When to harvest: Berries turn blue when ripe, but letting them sweeten on the plant for another few days is recommended. Gently twist, rather than pull, berries free.

Pests/problems: Blueberry maggots (larvae of adult blueberry maggot fly), birds and cherry fruitworms (tiny red worms that attack fruit). To control blueberry maggots, pick and destroy infested fruit. Trap adult maggot flies by hanging an apple maggot fly trap (a red sphere coated with a sticky substance called Tangle Trap) in bushes. Fruit loss to birds can be eliminated by placing netting over plants. Damage from cherry fruitworms can be minimized by spraying the bush with rotenone in the spring, after the flowers open. Picking all the berries, the good ones as well as the bad, will also help control future infestations of the fruitworm by eliminating some feeding and nesting habitat. Diseases that may infect blueberries are blueberry cane canker (characterized by red swellings on stems), a problem more prevalent in the South, and botrytis blight (a fungal disease evidenced by a brownish gray mold or brownish spots on fruit and blossoms), which can appear in periods of humid, wet weather. You must contain cane canker since there is no cure. Destroy infected plants and replace them with canker-resistant cultivars like 'Atlantic' and 'Jersey'. Botrytis also can only be checked, not cured. Remove and discard infected blossoms and berries. Improve air circulation around plants by moving containers to another location. When irrigating, keep water off foliage and fruit, especially in humid weather.

CURRANTS & GOOSEBERRIES. The English brought the ancestors of today's domesticated versions of both of these delicious berries to America. While the plants are gaining more fans every year, they are rarely found in the average home garden in this country. This is a real mystery since they are easy to care for. Both require about the same conditions, and most varieties are self-pollinating.

Why more gardeners are not enjoying currants is a mystery, since they are productive and easy to grow.

Types to grow: CURRANTS (REDS)—'Fay's Prolific', 'Improved Perfection' and 'Red Lake'; (WHITES)—'White Grape' and 'White Imperial'. GOOSEBERRIES—'Careless' (deep red, spineless), 'Pixwell' (pinkish red) and 'Downing' (green and sweet but with tough skin).

When/how to plant: Two-year-old bare-root plants are commonly sold, and these are usually one to two years away from bearing. Traditional practice calls for cutting newly planted bare-root currant shrubs back to a height of 8 or 9 inches so they can get off to a vigorous start the following spring. If you can find them, we recommend buying three-year-old bearing plants in containers. Neither currant nor gooseberry does well in hot summer regions, so they are largely limited to zones 3 to 7. However, placing containers in a northern exposure may work if you are in zone 8 or 9. Use the berry soil mix described on page 26 and choose a container at least 2 feet deep. Late summer or fall planting is advisable because the shrubs begin to leaf out early in the spring. Plant early enough to give the root system time to develop before winter.

Care and feeding: Gooseberries are more tolerant of shade than currants, but both seem to prosper in a half day of sun and light shade in the hot afternoon. Mulch heavily with well-composted manure, and you shouldn't have to feed the shrubs the first year. The shrubs have shallow roots, so the heavy mulch—and keeping the soil evenly moist—helps prevent them from becoming dehydrated. Both types of plants grow fairly straight, but currants are shorter. Gooseberries can reach 4 or 5 feet in height and can be trained to a trellis or wire. To contain the rampant growth of both gooseberries and currants, you need to prune the plants when they are dormant. Take out the old wood that has produced fruit to leave room for new stems.

When to harvest: Test currants for ripeness by pressing them between your thumb and forefinger. When they have a slight give, they are at their peak of flavor. Gooseberries are best picked when they are firm but not hard. You'll need thick garden gloves to harvest berries from all but the thornless varieties.

Pests/problems: Currants and gooseberries are attacked by aphids, currant borers, gooseberry fruitworms (which bore into and destroy fruit) and imported currantworms (which are the larvae of a sawfly that strips newly formed leaves from plants). Control aphids with insecticidal soap or rotenone. Prune out canes infested with currant borers and discard in the garbage. To rid plants of gooseberry fruitworms, spray the shoots and foliage with rotenone and remove all damaged fruit. Imported currantworms can be eradicated with a pyrethrin-rotenone spray.

Diseases that afflict both species are anthracnose (yellow-brown patches on leaves that quickly expand), gooseberry mildew (white powdery deposits on foliage), powdery mildew (white-gray areas, as if dusted with powder) and septoria leaf spot (leaves develop yellow spots and ultimately drop). Anthracnose and septoria leaf spot can be reduced by spraying with a copper solution. Gooseberry and powdery mildews can be eliminated with a lime-sulfur spray. The gooseberry varieties 'Bedford Yellow', 'Langley Gage' and 'Leveller' can be damaged by copper, so if they are afflicted with anthracnose or septoria leaf spot, spray them with the following solution: 1 teaspoon of baking soda and 1 teaspoon of pure liquid soap combined in a quart of warm water.

BLACKBERRIES & RASPBERRIES. These berries, fresh from the garden, are often far better tasting than the ones from the supermarket. Unless frozen, neither berry travels or keeps well, so fresh commercial varieties are chosen by growers for their ability to survive the rigors of long journeys, rather than for flavor. Many gardeners are reluctant to grow blackberries because of their tendency to "run" and, eventually, invade the entire garden. But growing erect types in containers prevents this from occurring, since neither their roots nor their canes touch the ground. When buying raspberries, keep two points in mind: (1) buy only certified, virus-free plants and (2) if you're growing reds and yellows, don't plant blacks or purples (or vice versa), since red and yellow varieties can pass diseases to their darker cousins.

Types to grow: BLACKBERRIES (ERECT TYPES)—'Alfred', 'Brazor', 'Ebony King', 'Lawton' and 'Raven'. Blackberries are most productive in zones 5 to 8, although some cultivars can be grown in zone 9 ('Brazor' is one). RASPBERRIES (REDS)—'Canby' (thornless), 'Heritage' (everbearing) and 'Killarney'; (YELLOWS)—'Fallgold' (everbearing), 'Golden Mayberry' and 'Golden Queen'; (PURPLES)—'Purple Autumn' (everbearing), 'Purple Success', 'Royalty' and 'Sodus'; (BLACK)—'New Improved Cumberland', 'New Logan' and 'Shuttleworth'. Raspberries thrive in zones 4 to 8. In the hot and humid South, a good alternative is the heat-tolerant boysenberry—a cross between the blackberry, raspberry and loganberry. Or try growing the everbearing raspberry, 'Southland', which was developed for southern gardens.

Given sun, good air circulation and even moisture, blackberries will thrive without coddling.

When/how to plant: Both blackberries and raspberries are available as bare-root plants, packaged like roses. They are traditionally planted in early spring in mild-winter areas and in early fall in the rest of the country. But for container culture, spring is recommended. Cautions about winter injury to blackberries don't really pertain to container growing, since you can store containers in garages or basements where the plants can be protected from hard freezes. Buy two-year-old Number 1 grade plants. Soak roots overnight in a bucket of water. Then, before planting, cut the canes back to a height of 4 or 5 inches and prune out any dead or damaged roots. This stimulates development of lateral roots and gets brambles off to a good start in the spring. Both blackberries and raspberries need to be planted in a container of at least 10-gallon capacity, although larger (15- to 20-gallon capacity) is better.

Care and feeding: Blackberries and raspberries are tough plants that don't require a lot of coddling. They are self-fruitful, so you can plant just one variety and get good fruit set. Both need an open, sunny location with plenty of space around individual plants for good air circulation. Keep soil evenly moist and well mulched while berries are forming and just barely moist for the rest of the season. Canes of both erect and trailing brambles can be trained on trellises or fences to keep fruit off the ground and to prevent trailing types from rooting where their cane tips contact the soil. Both can use a feeding of 10-10-10 fertilizer when they are setting flower buds and after they have fruited. To encourage the growth of new productive canes, prune out at soil level, right after the harvest, all canes that have fruited. If spring growth is vigorous, thin some of the new canes to keep the plant manageable.

When to harvest: Both types of berries are ready for harvest in late summer (everbearers will also produce a fall crop). Take berries when they have a slight "give" to them when pressed between thumb and forefinger and when their color is vivid, indicating ripeness. Leaving berries on canes too long after they've ripened attracts hungry birds and insects. So harvest mature fruit often to save the crop.

Pests/problems: Blackberries and raspberries, like a number of other berries, are heir to a host of pests and diseases, but our experience has been that few of these appear in small-scale container plantings, provided one starts with virus-free stock. Commercial growers and gardeners who have row plantings of berries among other crops are more likely to be subjected to one or more of the following plagues: borers (which lay eggs on canes), raspberry fruitworms (whose larvae infest fruit), raspberry sawfly larvae (which defoliate and weaken plants) and redberry mites (which attack blackberries and prevent fruit from ripening).

Borer-infested canes must be cut out and burned or discarded in the garbage. Rotenone, applied before buds open, is effective if it catches the grubs of these pests before they tunnel into canes. Fruitworm grubs are about ¼ inch long. As adults, they become tiny brownish beetles that destroy blossoms and foliage. If you detect damage from the adults, remove and destroy infested fruit and apply rotenone to plants. Repeat the application in one week. Raspberry sawfly larvae gather like aphids on the undersides of leaves. You'll see colonies of light green ½-inch-long worms. Applications of *Bacillus thuringiensis*, pyrethrin or rotenone can make short work of them.

Anthracnose is a fungal disease that produces purple spots on canes and foliage. Blackberries are more susceptible than raspberries, so be sure to plant resistant varieties. If plants become infected, prune off and discard canes and apply lime sulfur. Crown gall is a bacterial infection afflicting both raspberries and blackberries. It kills canes by inducing cork-like swellings in cell tissue, which destroy passages that transmit water and nutrients. There is no cure for the disease. Mosaic virus attacks purple and black raspberries and causes splotchy yellow spots on leaves. The disease eventually weakens and deforms the entire plant. There is no treatment. Uproot and destroy infected plants. Orange rust is not a disease often encountered in container culture (since its source is wild brambles), but it is lethal to blackberries and black and purple raspberry plants that contract it. The disease is characterized by orange pustules that appear on the undersides of leaves. Uproot and destroy any plants that exhibit symptoms and sterilize containers before planting in them again. Powdery mildew is a fungal disease usually induced by wet weather and poor air circulation. Fruit and foliage appear dusted with powder if infected with this disease. Remove infected fruit and spray canes with lime sulfur. Shop for resistant varieties. Raspberry leaf spot, another fungus, speckles foliage with black spots that turn gray. Infected canes die. Lime sulfur sprays can curtail the disease. Verticillium wilt is first manifested in healthy leaves that first wilt, then yellow and fall off. The canes die soon after. There is no known cure, and affected plants never recover.

STRAWBERRIES. Undoubtedly the most popular home-garden berry crop, strawberries are as easy to grow as they are tasty. Most types are hardy to zone 4, yet they produce well as far south as zone 8. There are even plenty of cultivars for gardeners in zone 9, ones that can take the heat and humidity of the Sunbelt. In recent years, true everbearers have been introduced that produce crops in spring, summer and again in the fall. Regardless of the variety, the best bargains are often bare-root plants, but inspect them carefully before buying. Their roots may be rotted due to overwatering or desiccated from a lack of water. It is best to plant bareroot berries as soon as they arrive from the mail-order source or the day you buy them at the nursery. If they can't be planted for a day or two, store them in the crisper of the refrigerator.

Types to grow: 'Shortcake' (everbearing), 'Earliglow' (June-bearing), 'Ever Red' (everbearing), 'Lester' (June-bearing), 'Lateglow' (late-maturing, June-bearing), 'Big Red' (June-bearing), 'Royalty' (June-bearing), 'Ruegen Improved' (alpine) and 'Yellow Wonder' (alpine, sweet yellow berries). For southern California and areas of similar climate, grow 'Aptos' (everbearing), 'Douglas' (midseason), 'Hecker' (everbearing), 'Sequoia' (early, planted in October, bears in December or January) and 'Tioga' (early).

When/how to plant: Set strawberries in containers in early spring in cold-winter climates. In warmer regions, fall planting is best. Gardeners in extreme southern parts of the country can plant through the winter. Use the planting mix recommended for strawberries on page 26. You can plant strawberries in anything from strawberry pots to hanging baskets. They can even be tucked around other crops, such as lettuce. Strawberry plants must be planted at the correct level, or they will rot or fail to produce. Build small mounds in the containers and set plants in the middle of these, taking care not to bury the crown, which can lead to rot. Mulch topsoil with plastic so that the fruits don't rest on damp soil. Strawberries prefer an evenly moist medium that drains well. A soil mix rich in humus usually provides strawberries with all the nutrients they need. Additional feeding seems to have a negative effect on production and texture. The traditional method of growing all but everbearers is to sacrifice the first year's crop for a bumper crop

New Zealanders named this fruit "kiwi," because the fuzzy, egg-shaped fruit resembles the body of their native flightless bird of that name.

next year by pinching out all flower stems the first season. This makes the plants more vigorous and long-lived since their energy can then be concentrated on developing a healthy root system. Flower stems on everbearing types are removed until July to give them a chance to gain vigor. As a result, their berries are usually larger and more plentiful. With bare-root plants, prune off any decaying or broken roots and stems before planting.

Care and feeding: Sun and plenty of water in a soil mix that drains well produce the best strawberries. In hot weather, tenting with shade cloth or row-cover fabric keeps plants from becoming stressed. Plants still producing late in the season can be protected from frost with hot caps or cloches. Beginning in their second year, most plants send out runners, or miniature versions of the mother plant. Removing these will return the plant's energy to fruit production. However, if you want to increase your stock of plants, you can anchor the runners in the soil with hairpins or bent paper clips until they root. They can then be cut from the mother plant and moved or left in place.

When to harvest: Take berries as soon as they ripen to prevent predation by birds and insects and to avoid disease.

Pests/problems: Fortunately, most plants grown in soil mixes in containers aren't threatened by the prevalent killers of strawberries—two soil-borne diseases called verticillium wilt and red stele (root rot). Pests that may attack plants include aphids, which, like spider mites, weaken plants by sucking sap, and spittlebugs, which produce a bubbly substance in which they live. Spittlebugs weaken plants by draining sap. Strawberry leaf rollers attack leaves then roll up a leaf to house their cocoon while they pupate. Strawberry root weevil larvae destroy roots and crowns. Aphids, spider mites and spittlebugs can be hosed off plants or controlled with sprays of soap solutions. Leaf rollers can be eliminated by removing rolled leaves containing cocoons. Root weevils can be killed by injecting parasitic nematodes into the soil. The three leaf fungi that infect strawberries—blight, scorch and spot—can be avoided by planting fungus-resistant varieties. A common fungal disease of strawberries is powdery mildew, which coats berries with a powdery fungus. Leaf undersides often turn reddish purple. Prune off infected portions and dust plants with sulfur. Keep irrigation water off foliage to prevent future infections.

Fruiting Vines

KIWI (CHINESE GOOSEBERRY). This desirable ornamental vine originated in eastern Asia (probably China) and was adopted by New Zealanders who dubbed it "kiwi," probably because the fuzzy, egg-shaped fruit resembles the body of their native flightless bird of that name. There are three species of kiwi that have gained popularity for their handsome foliage and tasty fruit—*Actinidia deliciosa* (formerly *A. chinensis*), a frost-tender type that produces the popular oval fruit found in many supermarkets and the lesser-known hardy kiwis, *A. arguta* and *A. kolomikta*, which bear fuzzless, grape-sized kiwis that don't require peeling. Most fans of *A. arguta* say it is sweeter and juicier than its bigger fuzzy cousin. *A. deliciosa* is frost-tender and hardy only to 10 degrees F. It bears showy but largely scentless flowers. It can grow to 30 feet if not headed back. Hardy kiwis can survive temperatures as low as -25 degrees F. They produce smaller, scented blooms. All kiwis are very high in vitamin C. The primary problem with *A. deliciosa* is the long wait for a harvest—up to six years with immature vines. *A. arguta* will often bear in its second season.

Types to grow: TENDER (*Actinidia deliciosa*, sometimes sold as *A. chinensis*)—female varieties include 'Chico' and 'Hayward' (both require 600 to 800 hours of winter chilling—temperatures between 32 degrees F and 45 degrees F) and 'Vincent' (which has a lower chill requirement of 300 to 400 hours). HARDY (*A. arguta*)—female varieties include 'Ananasnaja', 'Hood River', 'Meader' and USDA cultivars '74-8', '74-49' and '74-55'. EVEN MORE HARDY (*A. kolomikta*)—'Nahodka', 'Pavlovskaya' and 'Krupnopladnaya'. With the exception of an early fruiting variety called 'Issai', all the above are self-infertile, so a male variety must be planted with them to ensure fruiting. One male will pollinate eight or more female kiwis.

When/how to plant: Although kiwis can be planted any time of year in mild-winter regions, the most auspicious planting time seems to be very early spring—February or March—when they are available as bare-root plants. Use a standard planting mix with an additional cup of horticultural sand to each gallon of mix to enhance drainage. Use a half whiskey barrel or 36-inch wooden tub to grow kiwis. Because of the weight of fruit on mature vines, you'll need a sturdy trellis or other support to train your kiwi. You can use a fence or arbor, but the typical method is to sink two 6-foot-tall T-bar trellises into the ground and string two 12- or 14-gauge wires across the top, then train the branches laterally on the wires.

Care and feeding: Ideally, position the container in full sun and keep the soil evenly moist during the growing season. Mature kiwis need 1½ pounds of nitrogen each year. Young vines (those less than five years old) should get half of this amount. The nitrogen should be applied in three equal feedings, one in January and two more after the fruit has set. Immature vines that have not begun to bear fruit need to be fed only once in early spring and once in midsummer. Use a complete 10-10-10 fertilizer. Don't feed newly planted kiwis for at least three months. If you live in a growing area where frosts and freezes are the norm, don't feed kiwis after August to prevent the production of tender new growth that may be killed by frigid weather. Annual pruning is necessary to keep kiwis productive and thriving. New plants should be shorn of side branches until the leader (main vine) grows to the top of the support structure. When this occurs, hopefully in early spring, snip off the growing tip to force branching. Choose two vigorous canes to train on the trellis and pinch out the others. These two canes will produce lateral branches. When the vine goes dormant, head back the lateral branches to leave only four to six nodes (bud swellings) from last summer's growth. As the vine matures, continue to prune for better fruiting. Fruit will develop only on new shoots from the previous season's wood. During the winter, head back new growth to 16 inches, leaving seven to ten nodes per cane. These spurs will produce the next season's crop.

Pests/problems: Kiwis are almost pest- and disease-free. Japanese beetles may attack foliage. Cats are sometimes a pest, since they like to chew kiwi leaves. You may need to protect your vines with netting or wire. Make sure the soil drains well, or crown rot may destroy the vine by rotting it at the soil line.

When to harvest: Pick kiwis in late fall or whenever the skin begins to turn brown. Fruit will need to ripen indoors at room temperature. You can hasten ripening by sealing fruit and an apple in a paper or plastic bag. The ethylene gas produced by apples seems to speed up the process. Fruit harvested too soon will be tart. You can store freshly picked kiwis in the refrigerator for three or four months, then ripen them as described above.

Dwarf Fruit Trees

Growing your own apples, peaches, pears and plums will open up a new world of taste treats. You'll sample flavors in these fruits you never knew existed, since only a few of the many varieties of each that are available for the home garden are grown commercially. New cultivars are introduced each year from agricultural colleges and plant hybridizers whose never-ending quest is to produce the best-tasting, most productive and most pest- and disease-resistant varieties.

For the container orchardist, dwarf fruit trees are the best choice—the most productive in a limited space. There are two types of dwarf trees—*genetic dwarfs*, which are naturally compact, and *grafted dwarfs*, which have a rootstock that limits their size. (The scion, or fruiting part of the stem, is grafted to the rootstock.) One of the most dwarfing rootstocks for apples, the M27, produces a tree only 4 to 6 feet tall, yet it bears fruit of normal size. Also, because it is grown in a container, a tree's roots are confined, and this limits its ultimate size.

Virtually every kind of fruit tree—from apricots and apples to cherries and pears—is available in

'Dorsett Golden' is a low-chill apple variety available for southern and Sunbelt gardens.

bear more prolifically if a cross-pollinator is grown with them.

The ideal way to buy fruit trees is to visit a local nursery in early spring, if you live in a cold-winter area, or late winter, if you live in the Sunbelt, so you can inspect the plants before you buy. Also, you may have the option of buying balled-and-burlapped (B&Bs), bare-root or containerized specimens. But if you don't have a garden center nearby, or if you want to grow citrus and you don't live in California or the Sunbelt, you'll have to get your trees from a mail-order source.

Most long-established mail-order houses offer two- or three-year-old trees that they ship bare-root, when the plants are dormant. The roots are packed in moist sawdust, wood shavings, peat moss or other moisture-holding material and then wrapped in plastic. Most of the time the trees arrive in fine shape.

When ordering bare-root stock, check the condition of the roots when the package arrives. If any roots appear dry, the plants should be set in a bucket of water. If you can't plant the tree for a few days, wet the packing material and rewrap the rootball. Don't allow the roots to become dehydrated, or the delicate feeder roots will die and the tree will get off to a poor start.

How to plant: First of all, since fruit trees are a long-term investment, choose long-lasting containers in which to grow them. Redwood or cedar boxes, large clay pots or half whiskey barrels are all ideal. Most dwarf fruit trees thrive in containers with a capacity of about 15 gallons—approximately the volume held by a 24-inch by 36-inch box—al-

dwarf form, but not all varieties of a particular fruit tree are available. Still, there are enough dwarfs on the market to more than fill the desires of the most avid backyard or patio orchardist.

When selecting varieties, note that some need a pollinator (a different variety) planted nearby to produce abundant fruit. Unless you want to grow additional trees, choose, where possible, a cultivar that is self-fruitful. Even these, however, sometimes

Cherry trees produce in zones 5 to 8. Most varieties are self-infertile and need a pollinator nearby.

though they will prosper in larger or slightly smaller containers.

Pour in soil mix (see page 26 for the best mix for fruit trees) until the container is a quarter full, then drop in two slow-release fertilizer pellets, such as Osmocote Tree & Shrub Planting Tablets, and cover these with a layer of soil. Now, you're ready to proceed with planting the tree.

If you buy containerized stock in cans, have someone at the nursery slit the can for you. Trying to do this yourself can be dangerous to you and the tree.

Most nursery stock today is grown in plastic tubs. With these, it isn't necessary to slit the container. Instead, water the tree well, then lay it on its side and press down around the circumference of the container to loosen the soil ball. Then, stand the tub part way up and gently pull out the tree by its trunk. If it doesn't release with a *gentle* tug, water it again and press in the sides.

Once you have removed the tree, use a yardstick to measure its proper planting depth in the container. Ideally, the tree should be positioned so its graft of scion wood and rootstock is a few inches above the level of the soil and the level of the soil

is 5 inches below the rim of the container. This leaves room for a layer of mulch and for irrigating without washing soil out of the container. Measuring will tell you how much soil mix you have to add to have the tree standing at the proper height. Once this has been determined and the right level is achieved, lift the tree by its rootball not by its trunk. (If it is a B&B specimen, lift it by the burlap.) If the tree's roots have grown in a circle inside the pot, they should be carefully untangled and spread out before you transplant. Then, set the tree in its new container and gradually fill in around the roots with soil mix, tamping the mix firmly with your fist.

With B&Bs, fold the burlap back away from the crown. You don't have to remove it—it will degrade in the soil after a few months. However, if the tree is wrapped in plastic, that should be removed. Then add soil and tamp the mix as described for planting container-grown trees.

Bare-root trees are a bit more work. You have to build a mound of mix in the container, then splay the roots over the sloping sides of the mound. Begin filling and tamping down the mix until the soil level is about 2 inches below the graft union. It's best to replant a tree at its original growing depth. That depth is usually indicated by the line where the bark changes from a dark to a lighter color. (The dark bark was buried, the light bark was exposed above ground.)

Whether you're planting B&B, containerized or bare-root trees, never bury or mulch over the graft union. On dwarfed trees, you will see a hump with a healed-over pruning scar. This is the graft or bud union. If it is covered, the scion usually dies. A shoot may grow from the rootstock, but it will be of some unknown and less desirable variety.

When to plant: The rule of thumb in fruit tree culture is to get the roots growing before the top growth begins, otherwise the tree may perform poorly. This is why fruit trees, both bare-root and B&B specimens, are traditionally planted while they are dormant. The exception here is container-grown stock. Because the tree is growing in soil, it may already be at work sending out a new feeder root. So there is little danger of it weakening if it begins to bud out before you put it in its new container. Planting schedules vary drastically, depending on where you live. In California, Arizona, southern Texas and across the Sunbelt, fruit trees are planted as early as January. Planting times for the rest of the country are usually early spring, so trees can become established before the arrival of stressing heat, or early fall, which will allow a tree to adapt in its location and develop a vigorous root system before the advent of freezing weather. With container culture, spring is the optimum planting time.

Care and feeding: Fruit trees need plenty of sun—about six hours a day. Ample water is another requirement. Roughly an inch of water a week is adequate. This translates into about two gallons per container. If rain occurs frequently, wait until the mix dries out to a depth of 2 inches before irrigating. We've found that you can't overwater a vigorously growing fruit tree planted in a mix with good drainage. Overwatering is more of a concern with trees grown in the garden (especially in clay soil), where excessive moisture can collect around roots, inducing rot.

Fertilizer pellets in the bottom layer of soil in containers will sustain the tree for the first season. If you don't use pellets, you'll have to feed every two weeks with a 10-10-10 fertilizer diluted to half strength. You can also use fertilizer especially formulated for fruit trees in the form of spikes, which you drive into the upper layer of soil. Like pellets, these dissolve slowly through the growing season, providing adequate nourishment.

To help get newly planted trees off to a good start, we always prune all branches back by one-third. This reduces the demand on the young root system for water and nutrients. We also remove any branches that could rub together and create a wound or opening for insects or diseases to penetrate. And we always cut back any injured branches. When pruning or shaping apple trees, always favor retaining the lower branches. This is where most of the fruiting occurs in the first few years.

As your fruit trees mature, they will need periodic pruning and thinning to open the interior to light, to force fruiting on lateral branches, instead of just the tips, to encourage earlier blooming and to enhance the production and size of fruit. Each species varies slightly in its need for pruning. We recommend that you buy, or borrow from the library, a good illustrated book on pruning techniques for fruit trees.

Pests/problems: Healthy, vigorous fruit trees are

There are no dwarf figs, but growing them in containers and pruning selectively keeps them small.

less likely to be bothered by insects and disease than trees that are under stress. So try to keep your trees pruned, adequately watered and fed. Fortunately, trees grown in containers are rarely troubled by soil-borne pests and ailments that afflict orchard trees in traditional gardens. In fact, if you are growing only one or two trees, the chances of their being attacked by insects or diseases are much lower than with trees in a large orchard. However, it is always prudent to pick all the ripe, or overripe, fruit and to clean leaves and plant debris out of the containers. This removes potential habitat for insects and disease organisms. A general discussion of the major pests and diseases that damage fruit trees is included in Chapter 6.

Also, most mail-order firms include a guide on fruit-tree care with their shipments. For information on specific fruit-tree problems in your area, contact the county agent with your local cooperative extension service, who can often recommend preventive or corrective measures. Increasingly, agents are advising gardeners on the least toxic,

Trouble-free and precocious, pears are among the most rewarding fruit trees for container growers.

most benign methods for discouraging insect and ailment problems. We urge that you take those steps toward environmentally responsible solutions.

Gardeners in cold-winter regions will need to provide seasonal protection for fruit trees, especially cold-sensitive varieties in marginal growing areas. Container-grown trees don't have surrounding soil to insulate their roots, so they are more at risk when freezing weather arrives. The best solution is to wheel containers of dormant trees into an unheated garage, basement or cellar. You can also bury containers in the ground up to their rims and mound soil, peat moss, compost or other mulching material over them. Then cover this mound with plastic, securely tied to the trunk and anchored with bricks or rocks around the edges. It is also advisable to wrap a collar of quarter-inch mesh hardware cloth 12 inches high around the trunk of the tree to protect the bark from rodents. Where freezes are not severe or of long duration, simply insulate the pots above ground with a blanket of mulch and a plastic cover to hold it in place against strong winds. Sunbelt gardeners can leave containers where they are growing. Frosts rarely damage dormant trees.

APPLES. Many of the most popular apple varieties are self-infertile and require a pollinator that blooms at the same time to produce abundantly. Also, most apples have a chilling requirement—a set number of hours of *continuous* winter chilling below 45 degrees F. The average is 1,000 hours. If this chilling requirement isn't met, the tree may leaf out and produce a few blooms, but it will not set fruit. There are a number of low-chill dwarf apple varieties available for southern and Sunbelt gardens. Some of these are listed below. Most apples thrive in zones 5 to 8.

Types to grow: 'Empire' (cross between 'McIntosh' and 'Delicious'; recommended pollinators: 'Gibson', 'Golden Delicious' and 'Red Delicious'), 'Garden Delicious' (self-pollinating, yellow Gravenstein type), 'Gibson Yellow Delicious' (self-pollinating), 'Red Delicious' (recommended pollinator: 'Red McIntosh') and 'Red McIntosh' (recommended pollinator: 'Red Delicious').

LOW-CHILL APPLE VARIETIES—'Anna' (zones

8 to 9, recommended pollinators: 'Dorsett Golden' and 'Ein Shemer'), 'Beverly Hills' (zones 8 to 9, recommended pollinator: 'Ein Shemer'), 'Gordon' (zones 8 to 9, self-fruitful), 'Winter Banana' (zones 8 to 9, recommended pollinators: 'Red Astrachan' and 'Winter Pearmain') and 'Winter Pearmain' (zones 8 to 9, recommended pollinator: 'Winter Banana').

APRICOTS. In addition to bearing delicious fruit, the apricot tree is highly ornamental and long-lived. It produces lovely white flowers in early spring. It is among the earliest of spring bloomers, and this characteristic limits its range to zones 6 to 9. Freeze-killed blooms obviously won't produce fruit. Gardeners, particularly in zone 6, should be alert to forecasts of frost when trees are in bud or bloom. If there is a threat of frost, protect trees with a cover or by moving them into a sheltered location. Most apricots are self-fruitful.

Types to grow: 'Flora Gold', 'Garden Annie' and 'Moorpark'.

CHERRIES (SWEET). Most varieties prosper in zones 5 to 8 and have a moderately high chilling requirement; also, most are self-infertile and need a pollinator nearby.

Types to grow: 'Bing' (recommended pollinator: 'Black Tartarian'), 'Black Tartarian' (recommended pollinator: any other sweet variety), 'Compact Stella' (self-fruitful) and 'Garden Bing' (self-fruitful, a genetic dwarf that grows to about 6 feet high in containers).

FIGS. There are no dwarf figs, as yet, but growing them in containers and pruning selectively has a dwarfing effect on them. Although considered a tropical species, they recover from freezes and can be protected in winter by moving them indoors into a greenhouse or an unheated garage or basement.

Types to grow: The following cultivars are self-fruitful—'Brown Turkey' (medium-sized fruit, pink flesh), 'Mission' (black fruit, red pulp, does well in southern and Sunbelt regions), 'Peter's Honey'

Japanese plums bear larger fruits than more cold-hardy European types.

(greenish yellow fruit, amber flesh, bears in its first year and may produce two crops a season in warm climates) and 'Texas Everbearing' (brown to violet-brown fruit, pink flesh).

PEACHES & NECTARINES. Like melons, peaches and nectarines (considered smooth-skinned peaches) don't ripen and become sweeter after harvesting, they just become softer. This is why many commercial peaches and nectarines have so little flavor. Fresh, tree-ripened peaches, on the other hand, are wonderful, and the best way to sample one is to grow your own. Nearly all peaches (including the dwarfs and nectarines) have a high chill requirement of 600 to 900 hours, which limits them to zones 5 to 8, although this constraint can be fudged a bit either way. There are some peaches with a lower chill requirement, but they are standards like 'Desert Gold' (200 to 300 hours) and 'Ventura' (400 hours). There are also standard-sized nectarines that are low-chillers, such as 'Gold Mine' and 'Panamint'. Most peaches and nectarines are self-fruitful.

Types to grow: DWARF PEACHES—'Belle of Georgia' (late), 'Bonanza II' (midseason), 'Compact Red Haven' (late), 'Honey Babe' (midseason) and 'Red Haven' (early). DWARF NECTARINES—'Nectar Babe' (midseason), 'Red Gold' (late), 'Sun Red' (early) and 'Surecrop' (late).

PEARS. Pears are one of the easiest to grow and most immediately rewarding of the fruit trees. They are bothered by few insects or diseases, and the trees can begin bearing only a year or two after being planted, compared with four or five years for some dwarf apple trees. Unlike many fruits, pears are harvested when they are of mature size but still firm. Harvested pears can be stored in a cool, dark place, such as a root cellar or refrigerator. Remove them from storage a week or so before you intend to use them and let them ripen on a windowsill. All pears need another variety planted nearby as a pollinator. Most prosper in zones 5 to 8. Exceptions are noted below.

Types to grow: 'Bartlett' (zones 5 to 8), 'Bosc' (zones 5 to 8), 'Clapp's Favorite' (zones 5 to 8), 'Kieffer' (zones 6 to 8), 'Magness' (zones 5 to 8, bred from 'Comice', cross-pollinates with Asian varieties), 'Moonglow' (zones 6 to 8), 'Orient' (zones 6 to 8), 'Pineapple' (zones 8 to 9) and 'Seckel' (zones 6 to 8, resistant to fire blight).

PLUMS. Plums are an easy-care crop that produces abundantly, primarily in zones 5 to 9. European plums do better in cold-winter areas of the East because they bloom later in the spring, usually after the danger of frost has passed. Their fruit is generally smaller and sweeter than Japanese plums, but there aren't many dwarf varieties available. Japanese plums bloom early and bear larger, softer fruit. They are less hardy than European va-

rieties and are best grown in the warmer regions of the West, although they prosper in other areas with frost protection. Nearly all Japanese plums need a pollinator planted nearby.

Types to grow: JAPANESE VARIETIES—'Abundance' (red fruit, yellow flesh, recommended pollinator: 'Methley'), 'Bruce' (wine-red fruit, red flesh, early bearer, zones 7 to 9, recommended pollinator: 'Methley'), 'Burbank' (red-purple fruit, amber flesh, recommended pollinator: 'Methley'), 'Methley' (red-purple fruit, amber flesh, recommended pollinator: 'Santa Rosa') and 'Santa Rosa' (deep red fruit, yellow flesh, recommended pollinator: 'Methley'). EUROPEAN VARIETIES—'Stanley' (dark purple-blue fruit, yellow flesh, self-fruitful).

Dwarf Citrus Trees

There are dozens of evergreen citrus varieties that have been grafted onto dwarf rootstock or that are genetic dwarfs and are well suited for containers, either indoors or out. Most types produce fruit of normal size, and some bear the first year you set them out.

In areas where winters are harsh, trees may be brought indoors and grown as houseplants until spring. Many gardeners have adapted citrus trees to sunny indoor locations year-round, although most benefit from summering outdoors.

Types to grow: GRAPEFRUIT—'Marsh' (seedless), 'Oro Blanco' (sweet, acidless white flesh), 'Rio Red' (sweet reddish flesh) and 'Ruby' (red meat).

KUMQUAT—'Nagami'.

LEMON—'Meyer' (natural dwarf), 'Eureka', 'Lisbon', 'Ponderosa' (natural dwarf) and 'Sungold' (variegated foliage and fruit). LIME—'Bearss', 'Mexican', 'Persian' (*Citrus aurantiifolia*), 'Tahiti' and 'Rangpur'.

ORANGE (SWEET)—'Moro Blood' (blood orange, nearly seedless), 'Shamouti', 'Tarocco' (blood orange, reddish meat) and 'Valencia'.

TANGERINE (MANDARIN)—'Algerian' (more productive with a pollinator), 'Dancy', the leading commercial variety (seedy, sweet-and-tart flavor), 'Honey' (sweetest of the mandarins), 'Pixie' (seedless, easy to peel) and 'Satsuma' (seedless with a sweet, mellow flavor).

TANGELO (hybrid fruit between mandarin orange and grapefruit)—'Minneola' (medium to large fruit, more productive with a pollinator, as are 'Algerian' and 'Dancy' tangerines).

When/how to plant: Fruit trees can be grown

Citrus trees are well-suited to indoor cultivation. 'Meyer', the lemon variety shown, is naturally dwarf.

from seed started any time of year, but these will produce standard-sized trees of uncertain quality, which must be grafted onto dwarfing rootstock. For quicker, less troublesome results, buy young trees in early spring from a nursery or mail-order catalog and transplant them to containers. Containers for mature specimens must be at least 20 inches by 30 inches and preferably made of clay or wood, with several drainage holes in the base. If you buy trees in metal cans from the local garden center, have the nurseryman cut the can, then transplant without delay to keep the soil ball from drying out. Before dropping the tree in the container, we score the rootball with a mat knife, cutting in about 1 inch deep in three or four places. This may seem injurious, but it does stimulate the production of new roots.

Care and feeding: During the growing season, hot sunny days and nighttime temperatures in the low 70s produce the heaviest yield. Deep-water when leaves begin to droop, then let the plant dry out for a few days. Citrus roots must have lots of oxygen to thrive, and this is possible only when the soil is not wet. Feed with a commercial citrus food as recommended by the manufacturer. Most call for monthly applications, in diluted form, after the first season. Citrus often suffers from chlorosis (yellowing foliage), which is symptomatic of an iron deficiency. You can buy a chelated iron additive at the nursery to correct this.

If you intend to bring the tree to fruit indoors, you'll have to hand-pollinate. Use a small artist's brush to rub the bristles around the anthers (which contain the pollen) of an open blossom, then rub the pollen dust on the tip (stigma) of the pistil, which protrudes from the center of the bloom. Do this to every flower as it opens.

When to harvest: As fruit ripens.

Pests/problems: The diseases that afflict commercially grown citrus trees in orchards probably won't affect container-grown specimens. Insects, however, may. Both aphids and spider mites attack citrus trees and both can be hosed off. Heavy infestations of aphids can be eradicated with what is called superior oil or with insecticidal soap. Mites succumb to applications of superior oil or sulfur. Two of the most common problems with citrus trees are their blossoms dropping off and their failure to fruit. Successive cool days, high humidity and lack of sun are usually the culprits in both cases, but trees will continue to try to fruit if conditions improve.

CHAPTER 11

How to Farm Indoors

❧

S OME FORTUNATE GARDENERS HAVE BRIGHT ATRIUMS OR greenhouse additions that they can keep filled with vegetables, herbs and exotic fruit trees. Other gardeners in more modest circumstances raise crops of lettuce and herbs on a sunny windowsill. But for many of us, to grow a variety of vigorous, productive crops indoors, we will first have to raise the level of available light.

Gardening Under Lights

W e have reaped respectable harvests indoors by using fluorescent tubes with a wide-spectrum light that mimics rays of sunshine. Not only have we brought crops to maturity under grow lights, we have raised hundreds of healthy transplants, which we set outside as soon as the weather allowed. Being able to start seedlings as early as you want is a great advantage if you are trying to squeeze two crops into a growing season or if you live in a short-summer region and want to raise long-season crops.

A portion of a garage or basement can be transformed into a miniature greenhouse where you can grow small crop plants like lettuce, dwarf tomatoes and herbs entirely under artificial lights.

Various brands of fluorescent tubes produce different intensities, or lumens, of light—usually somewhere between 2,800 and 3,200 lumens. Generally, the higher its lumen count, the more efficient the tube. We have found that, for the price, the best way to buy fluorescent lights is in pairs of

*Fluorescent lights enable indoor farmers
to start seedlings early in the season.*

Plants for Various Locations

A warm greenhouse is the ideal indoor environment for virtually all crop plants. Next is a glassed-in atrium or sunroom, preferably with a large skylight, that shares the warmth of the rest of the house in winter.

In both these environments, you can grow just about any vegetable, herb or tropical evergreen. And you can grow subtropical fruits such as banana, grapefruit, guava, kumquat, lemon, lime, mango, natal plum, orange and papaya.

A south-facing window or kitchen greenhouse window will allow you to grow fast-maturing crops

one "warm-white" and one "cool-white" tube, each 40 watts and four feet long. They sell for less than $1.50 each and stimulate plant growth just as well as the far more expensive horticultural lights. Four-foot-long fluorescent fixtures with a reflector and plug, ready to install, sell for less than $10 at most building supply stores. While you are shopping, buy a length of cord or lightweight chain so you can hang the light fixtures and adjust their height.

For tiny seedlings, the lights should be suspended just a few inches above the seed-starting container. For larger seedlings, position the fixtures so the tubes are 6 to 8 inches above the foliage. For maturing crops, raise the lights up to 8 to 10 inches above the leaves and watch how the plants respond. If they appear to be "reaching" for the light, that is, getting tall and thin, lower the fixture a couple of inches.

Give crop plants 14 to 16 hours of artificial light each day. The cost of operating a standard four-foot fluorescent fixture adds only pennies a week to your electric bill. You can get double-duty from your light garden by growing flowering plants too. African violets and other gesneriads do extremely well under fluorescent lights.

Dwarf bananas grow rapidly and often produce fruit in less than two years from seedling plants.

and many herbs that don't require intense illumination. Among these are leaf lettuce, bunching onions (scallions), radishes, basil, mints, oregano and parsley.

Fruit Crops for Indoor Gardens

Indoor fruit growing is limited to evergreen species such as banana, citrus and papaya. Deciduous types, including apple, pear and stone fruits, need annual winter chilling to trigger bud set and fruiting. This simply can't be duplicated inside. The following are fruit trees routinely grown indoors under ideal conditions.

BANANA. These perennials thrive in a bright, warm environment, grow rapidly and often produce fruit in less than two years from seedling plants, depending on the cultivar. You can soon have several plants by carefully separating and rooting suckers (shoots growing from the base of the trunk) or by dividing underground rhizomes after the plant is well established. Even without fruit, banana "trees," with their long, ragged leaves, make novel and decorative house plants. They are self-fruitful, so you only have to plant one variety. Recommended cultivars include 'Apple' (short, plump fruit), 'Better Select', 'Dwarf Brazilian Apple', 'Dwarf Cavendish', 'Dwarf Mexican', 'Dwarf Puerto Rican', 'Grand Naine', 'Ice Cream' and 'Red Leaf'. Because bananas are tropical, they are very sensitive to cold weather. Foliage is killed by temperatures below 40 degrees F, but new growth emerges in warmer weather. Temperatures below 30 degrees F will kill the trunk. Each trunk lives about 14 to 18 months then dies after fruiting. Plants may be grown outdoors in a sheltered (out of the wind) nook that gets good sun all summer then brought indoors

before the weather begins to cool. Each hand of fruit requires about four months to mature.

CITRUS. GRAPEFRUIT—'Marsh' and 'Ruby'. KUMQUAT—'Meiwa' and 'Nagami'. LEMON—'Meyer' and 'Ponderosa'. LIME—'Bearss', 'Mexican', 'Persian', 'Tahiti' and 'Rangpur'. ORANGE—'Shamouti', 'Tarocco' (blood) and 'Valencia'.

NOVELTY CITRUS. CALAMONDIN ORANGE (*Citrofortunella mitis*)—produces abundant 1- to 2-inch strictly ornamental orange-like fruits. CITRANGEQUAT—produces decorative kumquat-like fruit, excellent in marmalade. LIMEQUAT (a cross between Mexican lime and kumquat)—pro-

Citrus crops, from grapefruits to limes to tangerines such as these, can be grown indoors under ideal conditions.

Orange blossoms will fill a greenhouse or sunroom with sweet fragrance.

duces yellow fruit the size of kumquats that are a good substitute for lime. ORANGEQUAT (a cross between orange and kumquat)—bears abundant ornamental fruit slightly larger than kumquats and not as tart. OTAHEITE ORANGE (*Citrus x limonia*)—a miniature version of a sweet orange, bears 1- to 2-inch fruits that taste like limes.

GUAVA. Red-fruited strawberry guava (*Psidium littorale littorale*), yellow-fruited lemon guava (*P. littorale longpipes*) and tropical guava (*P. guajava*) all make decorative additions to the indoor garden in cold-winter areas and to the patio or terrace in Sunbelt regions. Their fruit is often used in jellies and preserves, but they are tasty eaten fresh, either by themselves or in fruit salad. Guava trees have attractive foliage, bark and growth habit. Especially desirable is the tropical guava because of its sweet-smelling 1-inch flowers and yellow-skinned fruit, about the size of a large avocado. The flesh is usually orangish pink. Two excellent tropical cultivars to try are 'Mexican Cream' and 'Pear Guava'.

MANGO (*Mangifera indica*). The colorful (greenish yellow to orangish or purple-red) fruit, which grows 5 to 6 inches long and becomes quite prominent as it ripens, make the mango an interesting and dramatic candidate for the tropical indoor garden. Flowers develop in clusters and may be yellow or red. Three productive cultivars are 'Aloha', 'Edgehill' and 'Thompson Large Seedling'.

NATAL PLUM (*Carissa grandiflora*). Grown as an ornamental landscape and barrier plant in warm climates, the natal plum adapts well indoors with good light. It bears, often at the same time, white star-shaped flowers with a sweet aroma and 2-inch reddish, plum-shaped fruit. The fruit has a tangy, cranberry-like flavor and can be eaten fresh or used in jams, jellies or salads. Although self-fruitful, growing another variety and cross-pollinating by hand usually assures a bumper crop. Some cultivars have thorny spines. Recommended varieties are 'Fancy', 'Ruby Point' and 'Tomlinson' (thornless).

PAPAYA (*Carica* spp.). Easily grown from seed,

Red-fruited strawberry guavas make a decorative addition to the indoor garden.

papayas are ideally suited to a warm greenhouse or atrium. The plants may produce male, female or bisexual flowers. Both female and bisexual flowers produce fruit. If there are only female flowers, a plant bearing male or bisexual blossoms must be grown as a source of pollen. You can determine the gender of flowers by their shape. Males are tubular and roughly 1½ inches long with star-shaped ends or mouths; females are round and compact; bisexual types are tubular but narrower than males. Papaya plants are precocious and can bear fruit in their second year. Cultivars to try include the commonly seen HAWAIIAN TYPES—'Solo', 'Strawberry', 'Mexican' and 'Mountain'.

Vegetables & Herbs for Indoor Gardens

There is a host of vegetables and herbs that can produce well in a bright, warm interior. Following is a partial list of varieties to try.

HERBS (ANNUAL). Annuals grow for only one season and must be resown or replanted each year. Annual herbs that adapt to sunny window locations include anise, basil, borage, chervil, coriander, cumin, dill and summer savory. Parsley and caraway are usually biennials in indoor gardens, producing tasty greens in their first and part of their second years, then going to seed and becoming less palatable. Outdoors, they may be biennials or annuals depending on the climate and whether they can survive the winter.

HERBS (PERENNIAL). Perennials reach a peak of seasonal growth, die back or slow down, then resume growing the following spring. Perennial herbs that thrive in sun-drenched locations are: catnip, chamomile, chives, comfrey, horehound, hyssop, lavender ('Compacta' variety grows to about 10 inches, 'Jean Davis' and 'Munstead' to 18

With attentive care and a bright, warm setting, you can raise herbs, like this chocolate mint, greens and even cherry tomatoes.

inches), lemon balm, marjoram, mints, oregano, sage, rosemary and thyme.

VEGETABLES. We've had success with the following vegetables grown in a south-facing sunroom, glassed on three sides and with a large skylight: CARROTS—'Short 'n Sweet', 'Nantes Half Long' and 'Little Finger'.

CUCUMBERS—'Burpee Tasty Green Fl Hybrid', 'Carmen Fl Hybrid' and 'Fembaby Fl Hybrid'.

LETTUCE (LOOSE-LEAF)—'Black Seeded Simpson', 'Red Sails', 'Ruby' and 'Salad Bowl'; (BUTTERHEAD)—'Buttercrunch', 'Charlene' and 'Tom Thumb'; (CRISP HEAD)—'Marmer' and 'Minetto'.

ONIONS—all bunching types (scallions) and garlic.

PEPPERS (BELL)—'New Ace Hybrid'; (SWEET) —'Gypsy Fl Hybrid', 'Redskin Fl Hybrid' and 'Sweet Cherry'; (HOT)—'Anaheim TMR 23' and 'Long Red Cayenne Fl Hybrid'.

SPINACH—'Avon Hybrid', 'Lucullus' and 'Tree Hybrid'.

RADISHES—'Cherry Belle', 'Crunch Red FL Hybrid', 'French Breakfast' and 'Pontvil'.

TOMATOES—'Basket King Hybrid' (produces 1¾-inch fruit); 'Burpee's Pixie Hybrid' (produces 1¾-inch fruit on 14- to 18-inch plants); 'Florida Basket' (produces 1½-inch fruit on 4- to 6-inch plants); 'Florida Petite' (produces 1½-inch fruit on 6- to 9-inch plants) and 'Tiny Tim' (produces ¾-inch fruit on 15-inch plants).

Pollinating

Most plants depend on insects and, sometimes, the wind to pollinate their flowers for fruit set. When grown indoors, these plants need to be pollinated by hand. To do this, take a slightly moist cotton swab or artist's brush and dab the anthers of a flower to collect some pollen, usually a yellow, powdery substance. Gently rub the pollen onto the stigma of another flower. (The stigma usually protrudes from the petals.) Gather more pollen as needed and apply it to the stigma of every blossom.

A number of species, such as tomatoes, citrus and some tropical fruits, are self-fruitful and may pollinate themselves without the gardener's help. However, tapping the flowers to loosen and move pollen grains within them can increase fruit production.

Indoor Fruit Trees

Trees grown indoors follow the same growth pattern (flowering, fruiting) as they would if they were outside. Feed tropical fruit trees a 10-10-10 fertilizer in January, June and late summer. You can use a commercial citrus food for citrus trees. Citrus trees are subject to chlorosis (yellowing of the leaves between the veins and midrib caused by an iron deficiency). This can be corrected by either spraying young foliage with an iron chelate or applying it to the soil, where it can be absorbed by the roots.

In early summer, flush out undissolved fertilizer salts by taking trees outdoors and drenching the soil with water for several minutes. The process can be carried out indoors if a tree is difficult to move. Use a poultry baster to draw off water that collects in saucers under containers.

The ideal temperature for most fruit trees is, luckily, the same range that you probably find comfortable—69 to 75 degrees F. However, citrus trees prefer nighttime temperatures in the mid 60s.

Keep the soil barely moist. Don't let it dry out completely before watering. However, with citrus, water less frequently than you would other tropical and subtropical fruits. Citrus roots will rot in soil that is overly moist. The plants need plenty of oxygen, and oxygen can only enter soil that is drying out. So let the soil dry to a depth of 3 inches before irrigating. By keeping the soil slightly dry, you'll be rewarded with a profusion of flowers and fruit.

Citrus trees are often plagued with spider mites. These can be discouraged by misting the foliage when the air is hot and arid. Spritzing is also beneficial because citrus trees absorb moisture through their stomata (pores in leaves).

Pests are not a big problem with fruit trees grown indoors. Spider mites, scales, mealybugs and a few diseases may appear, but you can combat them with the organic measures recommended in Chapter 6. The most common problem encountered is mineral deficiencies. You can get advice from your nursery or agricultural extension office on how to diagnose and correct these imbalances that usually appear in foliage as discoloration, stunting or distortion.

All plants that receive light from only one or two directions should be rotated periodically. Otherwise, with reasonable care, your trees, herbs and vegetables should prosper. Our only caveat is that your collection of unusual fruits may grow and grow and soon you may be wanting to add a wing to your home.

Glossary of Horticultural Terms

AMENDMENT: A mineral or organic material, such as peat moss, manure, perlite, sand or vermiculite, that enhances the moisture-holding, nutrient quality or drainage properties of potting soil.

BARE-ROOT: Trees and shrubs that have had the soil removed from their rootball and their roots packed in moist sawdust or peat, then wrapped in plastic for shipment.

BENEFICIAL INSECTS: Insects that prey on plant-damaging pests but don't harm plants themselves; also, insects that pollinate flowers for fruit set. Some beneficials include ladybird beetles (ladybugs), braconid wasps, praying mantids and honeybees.

BORDEAUX MIX: A fungicide of copper sulfate and hydrated lime with moderate insect-repellent properties. It may be dusted on plants or mixed with water and applied as a spray.

BOTRYTIS: A group of parasitic fungi that cause plant diseases. Also, a disease caused by a particular fungus.

BUD OR GRAFT UNION: On trees, especially fruiting types, the place on the lower trunk where the scion is grafted onto the rootstock.

CROSS-FERTILIZATION/CROSS-POLLINATION: Fertilization of a flower by the pollen of another plant from the same or a related species, usually carried out by wind or insects.

CRUCIFER: Any member of the mustard family, including cabbage, broccoli, kale, cauliflower and horseradish.

CULTIVAR: Short for cultivated variety; a type of plant that has been bred or selected for particular qualities.

DAMPING-OFF: A fungal disease that causes seedlings to die just before or just after they emerge.

DIATOMACEOUS EARTH: Fossilized silica shells of algae called diatoms. Used as a dust to control soft-bodied garden pests.

FERTILIZER, COMPLETE: Any plant food that contains all three major nutrients—nitrogen, phosphorous and potassium (or potash).

FERTILIZER, ORGANIC: A plant food made from once-living matter, such as fish meal, manures and cotton-seed meal.

FUNGICIDE: Any substance that controls or kills fungal spores. Commonly used fungicides include bordeaux mix, copper sulfate and sulfur.

GENETIC DWARF: A tree that is naturally compact and grows, in most cases, no taller than 10 feet.

GENUS: A group of closely related species, a basic grouping or categorizing of plants.

GRAFTED DWARF: A tree produced by grafting a scion of another variety onto a dwarfing rootstock. At maturity, the tree will grow no more than 10 feet tall.

HONEYDEW: A sweet, tacky substance, mostly undigested plant sap, excreted by certain sucking insect pests, such as aphids and scales.

HUMUS: Well-rotted or decomposed vegetable matter, such as compost.

HYBRID: The plant resulting from a cross between two different strains of a particular species. Offspring from the first generation of such crosses are called F1 hybrids. Seed saved from mature hybrids will not usually produce plants with all the same desirable qualities.

LARVA: A worm-like or wingless stage in an insect's development; often the stage when insects are most destructive to plants. Caterpillars and grubs are larvae.

LEGUME: Any member of the pea and bean family that produces pods, extracts nitrogen from the atmosphere and gathers it in nodes on its roots.

MULCH: A layer of either organic or inorganic material spread over the soil to preserve moisture, to moderate soil temperature and to suppress weeds.

NODE: The place on a stem or branch where leaves and buds originate.

OPEN POLLINATION: Pollination by wind or insects. Mature seeds from open-pollinated varieties will produce plants genetically similar to their parents.

ORGANIC: Basically, anything composed of living or once-living matter.

PATHOGEN: A disease-producing organism.

PEAT MOSS: Mostly decomposed sphagnum moss excavated from ancient bogs; highly acidic and water absorbent.

PERLITE: A porous volcanic rock that holds moisture on its surface and is used in synthetic soil mixes to improve aeration and moisture retention.

PHEROMONE: A chemical signal emitted by females to announce a readiness to mate. These scents are used in traps to lure males, thereby disrupting mating and reproduction.

pH: A scale for measuring the hydrogen-ion content of the soil to determine its acidity ("sourness") or alkalinity ("sweetness"). The pH scale runs from 1 to 14. A reading of 7 is neutral. Anything below 7 is acidic; anything above is alkaline. Most vegetables grow best in soil with a pH of about 6.8.

SCORING: Making horizontal cuts across roots to spur new root development; usually performed when plants are severely pot-bound.

SELF-POLLINATION: The transfer of pollen from the anther to the stigma of the same flower or another flower on the same plant. A self-pollinating plant does not need wind, insects or pollen from another plant to produce fruit.

SPHAGNUM MOSS: A moss-like plant that grows in bogs and is highly water absorbent. It is used as a mulch, as a soil amendment and as a propagating medium.

STOMATA: Minute orifices, or pores, in the epidermis of leaves that enable a plant to absorb and expel oxygen and moisture (transpiration, respiration).

U.C. MIX: A basic synthetic soil mix developed at the University of California.

VERMICULITE: Expanded mica capable of absorbing several times its weight in water and nutrients; used as an amendment in synthetic soil mixes.

Sources

SUPPLIES

Biofac, Inc.
Box 87
Mathis, TX 78368
(Raises and sells beneficial insects)

Bozeman Bio-tech, Inc.
P.O. Box 3146
1612 Gold Ave.
Bozeman, MT 59772
(Beneficials, pheromone traps, soaps, biological pest controls)

Gardens Alive!
5100 Schenley Pl.
Lawrenceburg, IN 47025
(Organic pest and disease controls)

Garden-Ville of Austin
8648 Old Bee Caves Rd.
Austin, TX 78735
(Biological and botanical pesticides, beneficials, tools)

Great Lakes IPM
10220 Church Rd. NE
Vestaburg, MI 48891
(Integrated pest management products)

Harmony Farm Supply & Nursery
3244 Gravenstein Hwy. No. A
Sebastopol, CA 95472
(Large selection of drip irrigation equipment)

IFM
333 Ohme Gardens Rd.
Wenatchee, WA 98801
(Beneficial insects, natural insecticides)

The Natural Gardening Co.
217 San Anselmo Ave.
San Anselmo, CA 94960
(Tools, seeds, transplants)

Necessary Organics
One Nature's Way
New Castle, VA 24127-0305
(Beneficials, natural insecticides, makers of Concern Pest controls)

Peaceful Valley Farm Supply
Box 2209
Grass Valley, CA 94945
(Beneficials, large variety of gardening supplies)

Ringer
Safer Inc. (a subsidiary of Ringer)
9959 Valley View Rd.
Eden Prairie, MN 55344
(Wide range of natural products and organic controls)

SEEDS

W. Atlee Burpee & Co.
300 Park Ave.
Warminster, PA 18991-0001
(Free 200-page catalog, seeds, plants,
tools, supplies; one of the oldest, largest
mail-order nurseries)

The Cook's Garden
P.O. Box 535
Londonderry, VT 05148
(Wide variety of specialty vegetables
and salad greens; catalog $1)

Henry Field's Seed & Nursery Co.
415 N. Burnett
Shenandoah, IA 51601
(Free catalog of seeds, plants and trees)

Gurney Seed & Nursery Corp.
Gurney Building
Yankton, SD 57079
(Free catalog of seeds, plants and trees)

Hastings
P.O. Box 115535
Atlanta, GA 30310-8535
(Free catalog)

Ed Hume Seeds, Inc.
P.O. Box 1450
Kent, WA 98035
(Untreated vegetable seeds for short-
season, cool-climate regions)

Johnny's Selected Seeds
P.O. Box 2580
Albion, ME 04910
(Short-season crop seeds, supplies)

J. W. Jung Seed Co.
335 High St.
Randolph, WI 53957
(Free catalog)

Le Marche Seeds International
P.O. Box 190
Dixon, CA 95620
(More than 300 varieties of vegetables
and herbs, plus gourmet vegetables)

Earl May Seed & Nursery
208 North Elm
Shenandoah, IA 51603
(Free catalog)

Mellinger's
2310 W. South Range Rd.
North Lima, OH 44452
(Free catalog)

Nichols Garden Nursery
1190 N. Pacific Hwy.
Albany, OR 97321
(Free catalog)

Geo. W. Park Seed Co.
Cokesbury Rd.
Greenwood, SC 29647-0001
(Free catalog)

Seed Savers Exchange
3076 N. Winn Rd.
Decorah, IA 52101
(Membership organization dedicated to
preserving open-pollinated, heirloom
varieties of fruits and vegetables)

Seeds Blüm
Idaho City Stage
Boise, ID 83706
(Price list free, catalog $3)

Shepherd's Garden Seeds
6116 Hwy. 9
Felton, CA 95018
(Catalog $1)

Stokes Seeds, Inc.
P.O. Box 548
Buffalo, NY 14240
(Free catalog)

Territorial Seed Co.
P.O. Box 157
Cottage Grove, OR 97424
(Free catalog)

Thompson & Morgan, Inc.
P.O. Box 1308
Jackson, NJ 08527
(Free, informative 200+-page catalog)

Tomato Growers Supply Co.
P.O. Box 2237
Fort Meyers, FL 33902
(More than 150 varieties of tomato
seeds, supplies, books)

FRUITS & BERRIES

**Ahrens Strawberry Nursery &
Plant Labs**
RR 1
Huntingburg, IN 47542
(Virus-free berries and fruit trees)

Ames' Orchard and Nursery
18292 Wildlife Rd.
Fayetteville, AR 72701
(Disease-resistant fruits, virus-free
berries)

Banana Tree
715 Northampton St.
Easton, PA 18042
(Many varieties of banana, tea, coffee,
chocolate and kiwi for the exotic-plant
gardener)

Bountiful Ridge Nurseries, Inc.
Box 250
Princess Anne, MD 21853
(Virus-free stock)

Brittingham Plant Farms
Box 2538
Salisbury, MD 21801
(Berries)

E. J. Bryant
Washburn, WI 54891
(Raspberries, blackberries)

Buntings' Nursery, Inc.
Selbyville, DE 19975
(Strawberries)

Burgess Seed & Plant Co.
Galesburg, MI 49053
(Berries)

D. A. Byrd
Locata, MI 49063
(Blueberries)

Cedar Grove Nursery
Cove City, NC 27231
(Rabbiteye blueberries)

Chapman Berry Farm
E. Leroy, MI 49655
(Strawberries)

The Clyde Nursery
Hwy. U.S. 20
Clyde, OH 43410
(Fruit trees, berries)

Henry Field's Seed & Nursery Co.
415 N. Burnett
Shenandoah, IA 51601
(Fruit trees, berries)

Fruit Testing Cooperative Association
Nursery, Inc.
P.O. Box 462
Geneva, NY 14456
(Fruit trees and small fruits; distributes
varieties developed by the New York
State Agricultural Station)

Gurney's Seed & Nursery Co.
Yankton, SD 57079
(Hardy kiwi plants)

Lawson's Nursery
Rte. 1, Box 294
Ball Ground, GA 30107
(Old-fashioned fruit trees, more than
100 varieties of antique apples)

Lewis Strawberry Nursery
Rocky Point, NC 28457
(Strawberries)

Makielski Berry Farm & Nursery
7130 Platt Rd.
Ypsilanti, MI 48197
(Specializes in berries, also carries fruit
trees)

J. E. Miller Nurseries, Inc.
5060 West Lake Rd.
Canandaigua, NY 14424
(Wide selection of berries and fruit
trees)

Northstar Gardens
19050 Manning Trail N
Marine, MN 55047
(Stocks 33 varieties of raspberry and
carries nice selection of blackberries,
blueberries, currants and gooseberries)

Raintree Nursery
391 Butts Rd.
Morton, WA 98356
(Disease-resistant fruits, virus-free
berries and vines)

Rayner Brothers Nurseries
P.O. Box 1617
Salisbury, MD 21801
(Wide selection of berries and dwarf
fruit trees)

Savage Farm Nursery
P.O. Box 125
McMinnville, TN 37110
(Large stock of fruit trees, vines and
berries)

Stark Brothers Nurseries
Louisiana, MO 63353
(Fruit trees, berries)

DWARF CITRUS
Chestnut Hill Nursery
Rte. 1, Box 341
Alachua, FL 32615

Four Winds Growers
P.O. Box 3538
Fremont, CA 94539

Harmony Farm Supply
P.O. Box 451
Graton, CA 95444

Michigan Bulb Co.
1950 Waldorf NW
Grand Rapids, MI 49550

ORGANIZATIONS
California Rare Fruit Growers, Inc.
Fullerton Arboretum
California State University
Fullerton, CA 92634
(membership fee includes newsletter)

Indoor Citrus & Rare Fruit Society
176 Coronado
Los Altos, CA 94574
(membership fee includes newsletter)

Selected Publications

Better Homes & Gardens New Garden Book. Edited by the editors of Better Homes & Gardens Books.
Des Moines: Better Homes & Gardens Books, 1990.

Foolproof Planting: How to Successfully Start and Propagate More than 250 Vegetables, Flowers, Trees and Shrubs.
Anne Moyer Halpin and the editors of Rodale Press. Emmaus, Pa.: Rodale Press, 1990.

A Gardeners' Bug Book. Cynthia Westcott. Garden City, N.Y.: Doubleday & Co., 1973.

Organic Gardener's Handbook of Natural Insect and Disease Control. Edited by Barbara W. Ellis and Fern
Marshall Bradley. Emmaus, Pa.: Rodale Press, 1992.

Park's Success With Seeds. Ann Reilly. Greenwood, South Carolina: George W. Park Seed Co., Inc., 1978.

Rodale's Color Handbook of Garden Insects. Anna Carr. Emmaus, Pa.: Rodale Press, 1979.

Index